ethical space

The International Journal of Communication Ethics

Publishing Office
Abramis Academic
ASK House
Northgate Avenue
Bury St. Edmunds
Suffolk
IP32 6BB
UK

Tel: +44 (0)1284 717884
Fax: +44 (0)1284 717889
Email: info@abramis.co.uk
Web: www.abramis.co.uk

Copyright
All rights reserved. No part of this publication may be reproduced in any material form (including photocopying or storing it in any medium by electronic means, and whether or not transiently or incidentally to some other use of this publication) without the written permission of the copyright owner, except in accordance with the provisions of the Copyright, Designs and Patents Act 1988, or under terms of a licence issued by the Copyright Licensing Agency Ltd, 33-34, Alfred Place, London WC1E 7DP, UK. Applications for the copyright owner's permission to reproduce part of this publication should be addressed to the Publishers.

Back issues
Back issues are available from the Publishers at the above editorial address.

© 2022 Abramis Academic

ISSN 1742-0105
ISBN 978-1-84549-810-8

Aims and scope

The commitment of the academic quarterly, *Ethical Space*, is to examine significant historical and emerging ethical issues in communication. Its guiding principles are:

- internationalism,
- independent integrity,
- respect for difference and diversity,
- interdisciplinarity,
- theoretical rigour,
- practitioner focus.

In an editorial in Vol. 3, Nos 2 and 3 of 2006, the joint editor, Donald Matheson, of Canterbury University, New Zealand, stresses that ethics can be defined narrowly, as a matter of duty or responsibility, or ethics can be defined broadly 'blurring into areas such as politics and social criticism'. *Ethical Space* stands essentially at the blurred end of the definitional range. Dr Matheson observes: 'As many commentators have pointed out, a discussion of ethics that is divorced from politics is immediately unable to talk about some of the most important factors in shaping communication and media practices.'

The journal, then, aims to provide a meeting point for media experts, scholars and practitioners who come from different disciplines. Moreover, one of its major strands is to problematise professionalism (for instance, by focusing on alternative, progressive media) and highlight many of its underlying myths.

Submissions

Papers should be submitted to the Editor via email. Full details on submission – along with detailed notes for authors – are available online:
www.ethical-space.co.uk

Subscription Information

Each volume contains 4 issues, issued quarterly. Enquiries regarding subscriptions and orders, both in the UK and overseas, should be sent to:

Journals Fulfilment Department
Abramis Academic, ASK House, Northgate Avenue, Bury St. Edmunds, Suffolk IP32 6BB, UK.
Tel: +44 (0)1284 717884, Fax: +44 (0)1284 717889
Email: info@abramis.co.uk

Your usual subscription agency will also be able to take a subscription to *Ethical Space*.

For the current annual subscription costs please see the subscription information page at the back of this issue.

www.ethical-space.co.uk

ethical space

The International Journal of Communication Ethics

Contents

Special issue: True crime, ethics and the media
Guest editors: Barbara Henderson and David Baines

Guest editorial

True crime ethics: A timely interrogation – by Barbara Henderson	Page 2

Papers

Women's empathic interventions in true crime storytelling – by Ruth C. Fogarty	Page 4
A police-run true crime podcast: A comparison of justice in *State crime command - Investigations*, *Bowraville*, and *Phoebe's fall* – by Lili Pâquet	Page 14
The ethics of bearing witness: Subject empowerment versus true crime intrigue in Kim Longinotto's *Shooting the mafia* (2019) – by George S. Larke-Walsh	Page 21
Sympathetic or blame-worthy: The handling of ethical complexities in reporting on the victims of the 'Essex lorry deaths' by Dutch online-only news sources – by Ilse A. Ras	Page 28
Murder tales – True crime narratives between fact and fiction: A troubled relationship – by Nicholas Beckmann	Page 37
'I'm not a journalist. I don't think that I necessarily fall under the same rules that they do': Journalistic ethics in true crime podcast production – by Kelli S. Boling	Page 44
Websleuthing, participatory culture and the ethics of true crime content – by Bethan Jones	Page 52

Article

Curing an ethical hangover: A forensic examination of the potential of the post-true crime movement – by Nina Jones	Page 60

Book reviews

John Mair on *The BBC: A people's history*, by David Hendy; Sue Joseph on *Through her eyes: Australia's women correspondents from Hiroshima to Ukraine*, edited by Melissa Roberts and Trevor Watson; Matthew Ricketson on *Plagued: Australia's two years of hell – the inside story*, by Simon Benson and Geoff Chambers	Page 62

Editorial Board

Joint Editors
Donald Matheson — University of Canterbury, New Zealand
Sue Joseph — University of South Australia
Tom Bradshaw — University of Gloucestershire

Emeritus Editor
Richard Lance Keeble — University of Lincoln

Reviews Editors
Sue Joseph — University of South Australia
David Baines — Newcastle University

Editorial board members
Raphael Alvira — University of Navarra
Mona Baker — Manchester University
Jay Black — Founding editor, Journal of Mass Media Ethics
Shannon Bowen — University of South Carolina
Antonio Castillo — RMIT University, Melbourne
Saviour Chircop — University of Malta
Clifford Christians — University of Illinois-Urbana, USA
Raphael Cohen–Almagor — University of Hull
Tom Cooper — Emerson College, Boston, MA
Roger Domeneghetti — Northumbria University
Deni Elliott — University of Montana
Chris Frost — Liverpool John Moores University
Theodore L. Glasser — Stanford University
Paul Jackson — Manchester Business School
Mike Jempson — Hon. Director, MediaWise Trust

Cheris Kramarae — University of Oregon; Centre for the Study of Women in Society
Takeshi Maezawa — Former Yomiuri ombudsman, scholar/writer
John Mair — Book editor
Ian Mayes — Former *Guardian* Readers' Editor
Jolyon Mitchell — University of Edinburgh
Colleen Murrell — Dublin City University
Kaarle Nordenstreng — Tampere University
Manuel Parez i Maicas — Universitat Autonoma de Barcelona
Ian Richards — University of South Australia, Adelaide
Simon Rogerson — De Montfort University
Lorna Roth — Concordia University, Montreal
Karen Sanders — St Mary's University
John Steel — University of Derby
Ben Stubbs — University of South Australia
Miklos Sukosd — Central European University, Budapest
Barbara Thomass — Ruhruniversität Bochum
Terry Threadgold — Centre for Journalism Studies, Cardiff University
Stephen J. Ward — University of British Columbia
James Winter — University of Windsor, Canada

EDITORIAL

Barbara Henderson

True crime ethics: A timely interrogation

When is a good time to explore the many questions and dilemmas thrown up by the recent surge of interest in true crime? Arguably, if the genre is having a 'moment', it's a long one. Its history in journalism, literature, drama, radio, film and television, and more recently, the podcast, can be traced back as far as the sixteenth century. Rohrer (2019) cites *A warning for fair women* (1599), the dramatised version of the 1573 murder of London merchant George Sanders, as prompting many more playwrights to adapt true murder narratives in the centuries that followed – but it can be tracked even further, to Ancient Greece (Franks 2016) and the Bible (Punnett 2018).

Even in the twentieth and twenty-first centuries, critical acclaim is sparse. Between Truman Capote's *In cold blood* (1966) and the 2014 podcast *Serial*, true crime is largely viewed as 'a genre of cheap paperbacks with little literary merit and highly sensational, pornographic content' (Rowen 2017).

What brought about the change in reception? It appears to be not just the focus by true crime writers and producers away from the criminal and onto the justice system (ibid), but also something relating to the platform. When podcasting began to take off in the early 2000s as a medium, the sense was that its potential was limited and its days, like those of radio, were numbered. Yet just as the podcast saved true crime as a genre, so true crime did much to bring about the rapid rise of podcast consumption. Today true crime podcasts rank as among the most consumed, only behind comedy and news/current affairs,[1] a phenomenon which in the last decade also prompted TV channels to renew their interest in the genre. The first series of the US podcast *Serial*, which explored the death of Hae Min Lee in 1999 in Maryland, was downloaded more than 211 million times; Netflix's *Making a murderer* was its most-viewed programme in 2018; and there are dozens of dedicated true crime TV channels across the globe. *Serial* became a 'water cooler' subject largely because of its investigative journalism, which led to the dropping of all charges and the release from prison in 2022 of convicted Adnan Syed, for Lee's murder.

But the podcast genre, with its ease of access and production, allows the retelling of countless other stories – often challenging the 'dead white woman' trope so loved by the tabloid press. While more than 50 per cent of the overall podcast audience is male, the figures are nothing like so evenly split in true crime (Brandwatch 2018) where the audiences are predominantly female.

This is not new information – true crime readers are predominately always female, and now the accessible podcast allows the representation of women in ways that 'use the affordances of mass media to draw support from the public, effectively inviting the audience to perform as an alternate jury' and 'engendering change in judicial processes' (Pâquet 2021). Boling (2019) argues that true crime podcasts are impacting the criminal justice system in unprecedented ways and could challenge both criminal justice and media reform.

But proponents also are accused of complicity in the propagation and popularisation of narratives of female-directed violence and the visualisation of mutilated female bodies (Greer 2017). And as the true crime genre is treated as a ratings winner, concerns about responsibility and potential exploitation were recently renewed, notably with the Netflix series *Dahmer* (2022) and the UK Channel 5 series *Maxine* (2022), which led a *Guardian* critic to remind us that 'not all murders have much to teach us' (Mangan 2022). And Hulu's knowing comedy drama *Only murders in the building* (2021-2022), which parodies the true crime genre, its podcast producers and its fans, reached the Top 10 streaming charts in summer 2022 (ComicBook 2022).

And yet, one of the only attempts to topographise true crime – Ian Case Punnett's *Toward a theory of true crime narratives* (2018) – remains largely unaccompanied and unchallenged.

So, as we reach potential saturation point, it's unsurprising that ethics are to the fore in this edition, which expands on the Newcastle University conference 'Investigating true crime and the media' held online in June 2022.

Ruth Fogarty considers how women's empathic interventions in literature demonstrate the possibilities for an ethical true crime genre on all platforms. Lili Pâquet's previous research considers how the true crime podcast attempts to fill 'justice gaps'. In this latest paper, she evaluates *State crime command – investigations*, but concludes that the police true crime podcast seeks information from listeners without attempting to fill any justice gaps and, therefore, appears more useful as an advertisement of investigative procedure, a recruitment strategy, or a tool for tying up the loose ends of investigations. George Larke-Walsh centres on Kim Longinotto's *Shooting the mafia* (2019) to explore the ethics of bearing witness to testimony on true crime events and how producers can potentially create empathy outside the frame of victimhood.

Ilse Ras uses a combined content and critical stylistic analysis to consider the Dutch online media's representation of the 39 victims found dead in the back of a refrigerated lorry in Essex and how the various ethical complexities associated with trafficking and people-smuggling were side-stepped.

Via narratology, Nicholas Beckmann explores true crime's troubled relationship between fact and fiction, (un)reliability and trustworthiness. Kelli S. Boling turns her attention to journalistic ethics relating to copyright, and the ethical implications of plagiarism in an unregulated industry, with a focus on the popular podcast *Crime junkie*. Bethan Jones explores the participatory culture around true crime known as websleuthing, and questions the ethics of citizen investigation for real time cases on social media.

Finally, Nina Jones's extraordinary video essay explores how a 'post-true crime' movement responds with an attempt to redress and reframe the genre by re-situating victims' stories within the narrative and increasing the representation of stories from LGBT+ communities and non-white perspectives – and it proposes an ethical code for the genre.

It's too early to say if audiences, podcasters or TV producers have reached saturation point with the true crime genre, but as the phenomenon continues, these important considerations of the genre explore central ethical questions of twenty-first century popular culture.

Note
[1] See https://www.statista.com/statistics/786938/top-podcast-genres/

References and further reading

Boling, K. S. and Hull, K. (2018) Undisclosed information – *Serial* is my favorite murder: Examining motivations in the true crime podcast audience, *Journal of Radio & Audio Media*, Vol. 25, No. 1 pp 92-108

Boling, K. S. (2019) True crime podcasting: Journalism, justice or entertainment?, *Radio Journal: International Studies in Broadcast & Audio Media*, Vol. 17, No. 2 pp 161-178

Franks, R. (2016) True crime: The regular reinvention of a genre, *Journal of Asia-Pacific Pop Culture*, Vol. 1, No. 2 pp 239-254

Greer, A. (2017) Murder, she spoke: The female voice's ethics of evocation and spatialisation in the true crime podcast, *Sound Studies*, Vol. 3, No. 2 pp 152-164

Joyce, G. (2018) Podcast audiences: Why are women such big fans of true crime podcasts?, *Brandwatch*. Available online at https://www.brandwatch.com/blog/react-podcast-audiences/, accessed on 28 October 2022

Mangan, L. (2022) Maxine review – A show about the Soham murders that is both pointless and dangerous, *Guardian*, 10 October. Available online at https://www.theguardian.com/tv-and-radio/2022/oct/10/maxine-review-a-show-about-the-soham-murders-that-is-both-pointless-and-dangerous, accessed on 28 October 2022

Pâquet, L. (2021) Seeking justice elsewhere: Informal and formal justice in the true crime podcasts *Trace* and *The Teacher's Pet*, *Crime, Media, Culture*, Vol. 17, No. 3 pp 421-437. Available online at https://doi.org/10.1177/1741659020954260

Punnett, I. C. (2018) *Toward a theory of true crime narratives: A textual analysis*, London, Routledge

Ridgely, C. (2022) *Only murders in the building* cracks streaming ratings Top 10 but can't topple Netflix strangehold, *ComicBook*, 25 August. Available online at https://comicbook.com/tv-shows/news/only-murders-in-the-building-season-2-streaming-ratings-hulu-netflix/, accessed on 28 October 2022

Rohrer, M. (2019) 'Lamentable and true': Remediations of true crime in domestic tragedies, *Early Modern Literary Studies*, Vol. 20, No. 3 pp 1-17. Available online at https://extra.shu.ac.uk/emls/journal/index.php/emls/article/view/439/360

Rowen, L. (2017) *True crime as a literature of advocacy*, Honors thesis, Bellarmine University, Kentucky

Zeitchik, S. (2019) Does Netflix have a killer problem?, *Washington Post*, 21 March. Available online at https://www.washingtonpost.com/business/2019/03/21/does-netflix-have-killer-problem/, accessed on 28 October 2022

Dr Barbara Henderson
University of Newcastle, UK
Special issue joint editor

Note about the special issue editors

Barbara Henderson is an academic, writer and former BBC and newspaper journalist. After an early career in newspapers, she joined BBC North where she worked for 17 years, including an attachment to Radio 4's *Today Programme*. She left the BBC to complete a PhD at Newcastle University and now she is degree programme director for Newcastle University's MA in Media and Journalism. Her research interests include true crime and activist writing/art.

David Baines is a senior lecturer at Newcastle University. The primary focus of his research is on the journalism of localities and communities; changing journalism roles and practices; the structure, regulation and political economy of the local and regional press. He is a founder member (with Prof. Agnes Gulyas of Canterbury Christchurch University and Dr Rachel Matthews of Coventry University) of the Media, Communications and Cultural Studies Association (MECCSA) Network on Local and Community Media. He is exploring the roles that collaborative forms of journalism are developing within communities and developing understandings that are emerging about the value of those processes – independently from the products, the texts – of journalism.

PAPER

Ruth C. Fogarty

Women's empathetic interventions in true crime storytelling

True crime's predominantly female audience is well documented, and research published in the United States characterises true crime podcast fans as 'female, active, involved' (Boling and Hull 2018; Vicary and Fraley 2010). After the success of Serial, hundreds of millions of new, 'predominantly female' listeners worldwide sought longform nonfiction storytelling that captured or elaborated on their personal interests and expectations, resulting in new configurations in true crime. Yet prior to this rapid, gender-informed expansion in the medium, another shift in formula was underway in Australia's literary nonfiction scene, where a series of high value nonfiction books authored by women and published as True Crime, were already transforming the genre. Acknowledging the ambivalence of authors whose literary works are categorised as true crime, my research explores the ways that women are impacting its narrative and aesthetic conventions. In this paper, I show that in their complex world views, self-implicating strategies, and their readiness to centre victims and survivors, these Australian literary nonfiction texts foretold the true crime boom. This is a case study of women writers whose empathic interventions demonstrate the possibilities for ethical enactments of true crime.

Keywords: true crime, literary nonfiction, empathy, women, genre

Before the boom, there was a shift

> At this moment in history, we're witnessing a significant evolution of true crime narratives in popular culture (Murley 2017: 288).

> It is probably quite accurate to think of the canon as an entirely gentlemanly artifact (Robinson 1983: 84).

The phrase 'true crime boom' is commonly used in popular media to define the recent phenomena of true crime content populating digital television and podcasting (Telfer 2019; Weinman 2020), and the content commonly cited as sparking this trend are the American podcast *Serial* (2014), the Netflix documentaries *The jinx* (2015) and *Making a murderer* (2015) (Horeck 2019). True crime writer and podcaster Tori Telfer refers to this 'boom' as having been 'midwifed into being with "prestige" true crime' (Telfer 2019), her use of the term 'midwifed' signalling the gendered nature of the cultural production, as the creators and producers (and yes, consumers) of true crime media are – increasingly – women. By contrast, Hazel Wright's characterisation of the modern genre stems from the literary tradition as one that 'was grandfathered in by Truman Capote's 1966 *In cold blood*' (Wright 2020: 9) – a definition echoed widely in the field, despite the text having notably lost its credentials in Ian Punnett's (American) theory of true crime (Punnett 2018). Accompanying the digital expansion of true crime entertainment is a discourse among content creators, academics, critics and consumers evaluating the genre's many ethical problems. However, beginning at least a decade prior to *Serial*, Australian literary nonfiction books authored by women and published as true crime were already troubling the norms and tropes of the genre. These texts challenge reader engagement and confront archetypes with a range of strategies, underscoring the ethical tensions and narrative resistances recently explored in contemporary true crime content in both literary and digital forms. Viewed as a body of work, these Australian nonfiction crime texts act as forerunners to significant developments in contemporary true crime storytelling. The question this paper intends to answer is: how can Australian female-authored literary nonfiction be used to illustrate the possibilities of an empathetic narrative framework for creators (and consumers) of true crime on all platforms?

Genre trouble

> Texts ... do not 'belong' to genres but are, rather, uses of them (Frow 2014: 2).

Helen Garner, Chloe Hooper and Kate Wild are three Australian writers who have produced literary nonfiction texts exploring a violent public act or private trauma through a deeply personal reflexive approach. Published between 2004 to 2018, these texts demonstrate a range of affective narrative strategies which serve to destabilise or deconstruct true crime's conventions. Reading and reflecting on these texts in the context of recent cultural and scholarly debates about true crime, I identify some distinguishing narrative strategies. Aside from their categorisation as true crime, these texts are chosen for their wide acclaim and popularity with Australia's reading audiences, although there are other examples of women's literary nonfiction written in and around the true crime formula, published domestically, which also illustrate this argument (e.g. *The trauma cleaner,* Sara Krasnostein (2017); *Small wrongs: How we really say sorry in love, life and law,* Kate Rossmanith (2018); *Eggshell skull,* Bri Lee (2019); *The winter road,* Kate Holden (2021)). Crucially, the books cited in this essay are not marketed as archetypal true crime titles, and at the time of their publication would more likely be housed under 'Literature' in bookstores – despite each of them gaining awards for true crime writing, among other, perhaps more reputable, accolades. Significantly, none identify as true crime writers and in an interview with author Kate Wild, she says she was uncomfortable categorised as such for the publication of her first book for fear of being typecast, among other reasons (*Kate Wild interview*, October 2021).

Helen Garner: Between moral outrage and the urge to comprehend

Helen Garner's true crime book *Joe Cinque's consolation* (Garner 2004), focuses on the criminal trial of a young female student accused of intimate partner homicide. The book's subheading, *A true story of death, grief and the law*, flags the larger moral and social themes addressed in the text, to which the author lends the full weight of her subjectivity. Garner admits she is intellectually drawn to ideas and enactments of justice, and this is how she finds herself attending the young woman's trial. She also admits to less flattering instincts, and is candid about her private encounters of bearing witness: 'I wanted to look at women who were accused of murder. ... I needed to find out if anything made them different from me: whether I could trust myself to keep the lid on the vengeful, punitive force that was in me, as it is in everyone' (Garner 2004: 25). The book is named for the 26-year-old man who died from a drug overdose in 1997 at the hands of his girlfriend, Anu Singh. After being found guilty of manslaughter, Singh serves just four years in prison. Attending the trial not as an objective witness but as a 'passionate observer' (Eggins 2005: 122), Garner swings back and forth between moral outrage and an urgent impulse to comprehend what really happened. After voicing her initial revulsion for the 'damaged infant, the vain, frantic, destructive, out of control girl' (Garner 2004: 19) standing in the courtroom, Garner – an Anglo, middle-aged, middle-class grandmother – strives to collapse the otherness of this young, Indian-immigrant student with mental health problems, who is categorised by the media as manipulative, narcissistic and 'Prozac popping' (Fitzgerald 2004). 'Call that mental illness? She's exactly like me' (Garner 2004: 38), Garner writes in response to Singh's psychiatric condition used in her defence. When the prosecution presents as evidence excerpts from Singh's diary, Garner, herself a prolific private and public diarist, admits to a moment of recognition and near camaraderie with the accused:

> Surely, I thought, remembering with a shudder the reams of self-obsessed ravings that had flamed in the backyard bonfires of my life, a diary is the one place where a girl can indulge her unacceptable narcissism with impunity? (Garner 2004: 40).

Throughout the trial, Garner searches for parallels of understanding to resist the type of binary character portrayals that are the mainstay of courtroom narratives. Despite her self-confessed love of watching the courts and their scripted protocols, the author resists the dramatic plotlines and, instead, looks for insight in minor scenes and small exchanges. Moreover, none of the *actors* serve as token figures here, from lawyers, witnesses, family members, through to the accused and the deceased. Despite his physical absence, Joe Cinque is a vivid presence, in large part due to the stories Garner is told about his unblemished status as beloved son. She also shows him as a young man who made some poor choices, and who played a part in Singh's delusions.

Yet Garner does not conceal her deepening relationship with Cinque's family, in particular his mother, who becomes the moral and emotional hub of the text. Maria Cinque is not cast as the indistinct 'grieving mother' but as a sharply outlined person of passion and complexity, her clarity and conviction a counter to Garner's own struggles with partiality. Maria's bereavement colours everything, and despite Garner's ambition to write a true story about the ethics of the law and the function and failures of justice, her insights are constructed in proximity to intense maternal loss. After publication, Garner was criticised for building a naïve 'framework of good versus evil' (Maher et al. 2004: 234) due to her undisguised affiliation with the Cinques and an absence of any equivalent voices speaking up for Singh:

Ruth C. Fogarty

The morality play script Garner adheres to closes off any nuanced understanding of crime or the criminal justice system. In the framework provided by the binary construction of good and evil, the idea that Cinque might have died a wholly undeserved death at the hands of someone whose guilt is diminished by virtue of abnormality of mind cannot be countenanced (Maher et al. 2004: 234).

Despite Singh's daily appearance in the courts, Garner fails to present her with the same complexity as her victim, and this narrative ellipsis is compounded by the defendant's legal right to silence – a facet of the law which openly frustrates the writer. Instead, Garner turns this 'research gap' into a feature, keeping the accused at a remove, imagining her way into the young woman's head, and again failing (Rossmanith 2014: 109). In an essay titled 'I' written in 2002, Garner explains her process of trying to understand and write about unknown others:

> The deal is this: if I'm rough on myself, it frees me to be rough on others as well. I stress the unappealing, mean, aggressive, unglamorous aspects of myself as a way of lessening my anxiety about portraying other people as they strike me. I have learnt, to my cost, that this will not always stand up in court. The intimate involves other people. But where do I end and other people begin? (Garner 2002)

Garner does not mask her bias against Singh, even while she admits at times a strong identification with her (B. Brennan 2017: 209), a bias which Singh has since criticised in interviews with the media after her release from prison (Adams 2004). In *A writing life*, Bernadette Brennan's biography of Garner's writing, we come to understand the author's anguished attempts to find an ethical place to stand to capture the emotional truth of the case. Writing in her journal, Garner describes her 'clashing thoughts' as 'sick with pity for the Cinques, sorry for the Singhs, curiosity about Anu' (B. Brennan 2017: 211). Eventually, Garner lands on a strategy that might encapsulate all of it, one which Brennan describes as 'a voice which dances between a troubled, observing first-person self and a more detached, authorial third-person' (ibid: 211-212). This subjective-empathic construct enriches Garner's nonfiction writing, even when – as critics note – it gets in the way of the legal facts (Maher et al. 2004). Ultimately, Garner cannot tell 'both sides', and the asymmetry is intensified by Maria's moral pull. This is a facsimile of another perceived narrative wrongdoing for her controversial nonfiction inquiry into sexual harassment, *The first stone* (1995), that 'seething site of defamation anxiety' (Garner 1997: 20) for which the author paid a heavy price. In *Joe Cinque*, Garner's ethical tussles are stand-ins for the readers' own, and her failures of objectivity reveal something truthful about the incomprehensible nature of the crime, absolving the author-as-mediator from her 'significant failure to provide a meaningful context for this crime' (Maher et al. 2004: 234). Garner tells the story of her first direct encounter with Maria in the women's bathroom at Melbourne court during the trial as the moment that sealed the book's fate. Seizing the opportunity to ask for permission to tell her son's story, Garner understood Maria's consent to mean she could no longer play the part of the detached witness. Seeing the Cinques failed by the justice system because of Singh's too-short sentence, and becoming so entangled in a mother's grief, Garner offers up this book as a gesture of moral restoration, a small consolation, for their loss.

In her next nonfiction book, *This house of grief: The story of a murder trial* (Garner 2014), Garner is enmeshed in another complex crime and punishment narrative. Here again, the author trades in the 'transmission of affect' (T. Brennan 2004: 18) by capturing her shifting mindset during the trial of a father accused of killing his three children. At first Garner refuses to believe this 'dull, lonely, broken-hearted man' (Garner 2014: 84), Robert Farquharson, is a monster or murderer – a position she shares with his former wife, Cindy, who defends her ex during the first trial. As Garner works hard to try to understand the 'sad father…in the shit car' (Garner 2014: 330), she reveals to the reader 'the loneliness of the monster and the cunning of the innocent' (Gornick 2002: 35). This time, Garner has made no emotional pact to the grieving families, and so she is free to immerse herself in the shifting dynamics in the courtroom, closely watching the wounded families, the faithful jurors and the performing lawyers. Garner as writer-witness-mediator captures the affects of atmosphere and emotion in 'the House' as Farquharson's trials and appeals extend throughout seven years. The exertion of paying attention over a long timeline, of urgently needing to 'find out why men kill their children' (B. Brennan 2017: 249), becomes a weighty undertaking. When Garner's grip on certainty begins to recede, it takes with it her last hope of the journalist's detached view:

To have my residual fantasies of his innocence dismantled ... filled me with an emotion I had no name for, though it felt weirdly like shame. ... I was straining to hold it at bay. I wanted to think like a juror, to wait for all the evidence, to hold myself in a state where I could still be persuaded by argument. (Garner 2014: 108)

When Farquharson is found guilty on three counts of murder and receives a thirty-three-year sentence, Garner comes to understand that nothing about such a morally incomprehensible act could be settled in the courts, and everyone will go on living in 'an abyss of suffering where guilt or innocence have no purchase' (Garner 2014: 50). 'What was the point?' she asks. 'What was the truth?: Whatever it was, it seemed to reside in some far-off, shadowy realm of anguish, beyond the reach of words and resistant to the striving of the intellect' (Garner 2014: 319).

Despite her deep reverence for 'the House', Garner knows the legal processes have failed to uncover what really happened that night; and she also knows her subjective study is not a locus for truth. Instead, Garner has written a testimony to the aspirations and fallibilities of the law, and the complex humanity enfolded in its institutions.

Central to Garner's writing practice are her experiments with the rules of literary nonfiction, and her interest in real life crime is something she has examined in public and in private (B. Brennan 2017). Her application of true crime's narrative structure – a murder, a trial, a sentence – is shaped by her subjective engagement with the difficult human experiences at the centre of her stories. 'The sorts of crimes that interest me are not the ones committed by psychopaths,' she writes to explain her curiosity about the Farquharson trial:

I'm interested in apparently ordinary people who, under life's unbearable pressure, burst through the very fine membrane that separates our daylight selves from the secret darkness that lives in every one of us. (Garner 2015)

About her nonfiction crime books, Garner is explicit in her intention to defy true crime's conventions, to tease out its affective power and in some way salvage its storytelling potential:

I think my main purpose in writing about murder trials is to tear these stories out of the trashy grip the tabloids have on them. I want to recount them in a way that gives full value to the psychological complexity of the accused person's actions – also of the behaviour of the judges and jurors and counsel. (Garner 2017: 57)

Few Australian authors have accomplished more than Garner in terms of reinventing the genre and enlarging its impact and reach.

Chloe Hooper: Challenging the true crime formula

Another Australian nonfiction text which significantly challenges the true crime formula is *The tall man: Death and life on Palm Island*, by Chloe Hooper (2008). The story focuses on the death in custody of an Aboriginal man, Cameron Doomadgee, at the hands of a white Australian police officer and the destructive repercussions that follow among the small island community off the coast of Queensland. Hooper was working as a journalist when she was invited to report on the trial by the lawyer representing Doomadgee's family. Hooper, a non-Indigenous Australian, travelled to the island for the trial and stayed with the story for several years. 'I wondered what I was doing here' (ibid: 33), she writes at the beginning. Having no prior insight into the Indigenous experience, Hooper quickly becomes alert to the smallest signs of tension and dispute with the policing and legal systems that shape their lives: 'For the Doomadgees, as for many Indigenous families, to be drawn into the law was to be drawn into an impenetrable labyrinth, all walls and no exits' (ibid: 47). Speaking with a white former police inspector, Hooper is thrown by his deep sense of connection to the island and its community and she sets out hard questions for him that she is unable to ask:

Can you step into this dysfunction and desperation and not be corrupted in some way? In a community of extreme violence, are you too forced to be violent? If you are despised, as the police are, might you not feel the need to be despicable sometimes? (ibid: 72)

During the trial, Hooper silently asks questions of Chris Hurley, the policeman accused of bringing about Doomadgee's death:

Do you ever dream of Cameron Doomadgee?

What do you think of the place you once chose to live, where good and bad are blurred and where you thought you were good?

Do you still think you were? (ibid: 190)

Ruth C. Fogarty

In court, Hurley turns his head and catches the author staring intensely back at him. Feeling herself exposed and chastened, Hooper quickly averts her eyes. Here she describes the rising sense of self-doubt revealing the author's uncertainty about her part in the events:

> I don't know if he knew who I was; I suspect he did. With a weak smile I turned away, feeling my blood surge. I did not have it in me to stare back. He was a man trying to save his life and he seemed to be saying, 'How dare you judge me?' (ibid)

As she peels away at the deep layers of hurt, doubt and betrayal experienced by the deceased's family, Hooper is unable to lean on her journalist's impartiality. Moreover, in learning about the long and painful history of colonial trauma which fuelled the death of Doomadgee and damaged the Palm Island community, Hooper must reconcile with some hard truths: 'I had wanted to know more about my country,' she concludes 'and now I did – now I knew more than I wanted to' (ibid: 214). As a self-implicating witness, Hooper knows that she is unwilling and unqualified to speak for either side, and instead she makes space for the anguished voices of the dead man's family and his morally injured community.

In *The Arsonist: A mind on fire* (Hooper 2020), Hooper revisits the 2009 *Black Saturday* fires that burned almost half a million hectares across the state of Victoria. In it, she strives to comprehend the motive of the intellectually disabled man responsible for lighting the blaze which killed 173 people and injured hundreds more – as well as extinguishing more than one million animals. Hooper conveys the devastated scene by channelling the voices of those who survived the visceral horrors of an inferno that was likened to 1,500 atomic bombs. Assembling the still raw recollections of those who lost partners, children, animals and homes, Hooper disappears and cites directly from their first-person anguish. Meticulously tracing the complex investigation into how and by whom the fires were lit, Hooper rarely strays from the impact of this large-scale devastation. There are few Australian residents who haven't in some way experienced the impact, directly or otherwise, of bushfires, and there is in general a shared respect for anyone who lives through the horrors wrought by proximity to a catastrophic fire event. Hooper channels this reverence for those who endured *Black Saturday*, as much as for those who do the painstaking work to understand and investigate the origins and causes of wildfires. In *The arsonist*, the act of catching the fire lighter, 'a misfit named Brendan Sokaluk' (ibid: 173), matters less than trying to understand his motives and Hooper consciously resists the law's attempts at oversimplification: 'The legal contest had pitted the story of a fiend against that of a simpleton. But the two weren't mutually exclusive. Brendan was both things: guileful and guileless; shrewd and naïve' (ibid: 158). The culprit is hapless and ineffectual, and he is also capable of annihilating families, wildlife and entire forests. Even with all the available evidence, the personal testimonies, the investigation and the trial, Hooper accepts her inability to comprehend the arsonist and, despite her deep inquiry, his crime:

> I have spent years trying to understand this man and what he did. My own motivations sometimes as indecipherable as his. And, I wondered, what if, having asked the police and lawyers dozens of questions, trying to get tiny details right, I essentially ended up with little more than a series of impressions? Would the result be ultimately a fiction? (ibid: 162)

In *The arsonist* and *The tall man*, Hooper resists satisfactory endings or anything that signals narrative closure. Instead, she deftly subverts true crime's reductive framing by asking the reader to sit with uncertainty and the discomfort of not understanding, at the same time asking us to acknowledge the complex histories, nuanced identities, ambiguous actions, and painful experiences of the individuals and communities at the centre of real events.

Kate Wild: Redefining the true crime genre

In *Waiting for Elijah* (Wild 2018), Kate Wild revisits the fatal shooting by police of a young, Anglo man in the grip of a mental health episode. She looks to everyone involved to understand how and why his death takes place. Through years of immersion in coronial inquiries, through conversations with police, legal and medical professionals, and through countless conversations with Elijah's family, Wild tries to make sense of what happened. Despite her professional credentials as a journalist and reporter, she is unable to formulate a clearcut narrative or construct a satisfying ending using the facts of the case alone. It's only when she implicates herself – as a witness, a mediator, and as someone who also lives with mental health challenges – that Elijah's story begins to take shape. Driven by her deep empathy for her subject and his family, Elijah's story becomes a catalyst for Wild to explore her own, yet she also fears the consequences: 'If I told my story with Elijah's, I would be labelled. The phrase "mental illness" in conversation was the verbal equivalent of Elijah's bread knife – an ordinary object, able to strike fear' (ibid: 169). Wild points to the stigma of mental illness as the larger context for her inquiry, marking a shift in the narrative and allowing the real interrogation to occur: 'In the right circumstances, what happened to Elijah – it could have been my family. … Sometimes I think it could have been me' (ibid: 184). In challenging the reader to consider the complex experience and prevalence of mental illness, Wild seeks to create meaning from Elijah's death. The author's search for understanding fuels the narrative, propelling the reader beyond the conventional signposts of an ending. When the coronial process is over, when all the legal protocols have come to an end and there are still no answers, the journalist continues her investigation. But now the urgency has intensified, as Elijah's story is entangled with the author's own. When the policeman accused of shooting Elijah walks away from the court without giving evidence or offering an explanation as to why he did it, Wild despairs: 'I wanted to chase him and pull at the skin of his face to force an emotion out' (ibid: 292). Wild continues looking for answers long after Elijah's parents divorce, re-partner and, in the case of Elijah's mother, after she develops cancer and dies. At times this approach appears to come at a cost. Yet it's through her intimate and personalised quest for knowledge that Wild's investigation is transformed into a highly affective and empathetic narrative – one with the potential to expand the reader's understanding.

In *Waiting for Elijah,* as in all these nonfiction texts, the narrator is transformed from investigator to emotionally invested autoethnographer, whose subjectivity gets interwoven into the storylines, collapsing the gap between witness, mediator and participant. For the families and communities at the centre of these narratives there is no closure, and for the storytellers any conventional attempts at constructing a final act eludes them: 'Why couldn't I make this story end?' pleads Wild on page 268. In an interview conducted after the book's publication, the author admits the toll of trying to reach a conclusion: 'I wanted to be able to find an end to the story, so I could end the pain I was in as a witness to the story. I learned a valuable lesson' (Shute 2018). In coming to terms with the impossibility of knowing the absolute truth or finding an ending, in highlighting the complications inherent in our policing, legal and welfare systems, and in showing her vulnerabilities and fears around her own mental health, Wild is interrogating and redefining the true crime genre.

Reimagining the genre

The genre relies upon the operation of sympathetic participation, upon affect, in narratives driven towards answers, illuminations and closures that are never fully achieved. (Smith 2008: 28)

In her 2008 exploration of true crime, Jean Murley describes the archetypal American 'murder narrative' as 'rigid, formulaic, predictable, and almost boring' (Murley 2008: 2), 'atavistic in its intensely gendered appeal and misogynist subject matter and avoidance of race and multiculturalism' (ibid: 3), and one which stands as 'a countercurrent to the social progress and cultural changes' of the times (ibid). This case study of Australian literary nonfiction crime illustrates some of the ways women are rewriting the 'murder narrative' as a storytelling model built on empathy and self-inquiry, one which assembles the facts while acknowledging the difficulties in knowing them, and one that can serve as a framework for mirroring social progress and cultural change. To identify this gendered reimagining of true crime, I have located the following narrative and aesthetic characteristics:

- Centring victims, survivors and those with lived experience.

- Seeking intimacy and subjectivity, more personalising and less objectifying.

- Asking questions of self and society, with less focus on *whodunnit* and more on *why*.

- Articulating doubts and expressing private fears and experiences.

- Emphasising narrative ambiguities and complexities.

- Questioning the meaning of guilt.

- Querying the role, value and the cost of justice.

- Challenging the possibility of finding truth and recognising there may be more than one.

- Resisting conclusions and neat endings.

- Demystifying the perpetrators.

- Confronting gendered, domestic and family violence – less focus on random violent acts from unknown perpetrators.

Ruth C. Fogarty

- Including racial, social and cultural diversity – more marginalised and silenced communities.
- Contemplating the aftermath of crime or violence.
- Acknowledging the moral and ethical implications of creating true crime.

Empathic framework in action

Table 1 is a demonstration of how certain empathic narrative practices can be mapped against the cited texts.

Table 1: Empathetic narrative practices in the texts

CHARACTERISTICS & COMMENTS	TEXTUAL EXAMPLES
– Victims and survivors – Intimacy and subjectivity – Questions of self, doubts and fears – Moral and ethical implications Garner's response to the victim's mother and her all-consuming grief illustrates the author's deep, personal connection to and empathy for the Cinques. The author's self-interrogation shows the uncertainties and concerns pushing against her overriding sense of moral responsibility to tell their 'story'.	**GARNER: *Joe Cinque's consolation*** For several minutes there was nothing on the line but the sound of her weeping. I was dumb with shame. How could I have thought that when I couldn't bend the story to my will I could just lay it down, apologise for the inconvenience caused, and walk away? Her son's murder was not an opportunity for me to speculate on images of disharmony and disintegration. It was not a convenient screen on which I could project sorrows of my own that I was too numb to feel. It was not even 'a story'. It was real. It was the brutal hand that fate had dealt her. It was the unendurable that she had to endure. Never in my life had I felt so weak, so vain, so stupid. (Garner, 2004: 270)
– Victims and survivors – Intimacy and subjectivity – Questions of self and society – Ambiguities and complexities – Querying guilt, justice and truth – No (neat) endings – Demystifying perpetrators – Gendered, domestic, and family violence Here we see the author grappling with the complexities of broken families and the tragedy of retaliatory violence wrought by ordinary men. Garner comes to see everyone caught up in this intolerable calamity – including the perpetrator himself – as a victim. Despite her willingness to bear witness to years of legal entanglements, she concedes that the institutions designed to argue and resolve matters of morality, truth and guilt can never close the fissure caused by familicide.	**GARNER: *This house of grief*** Farquharson's silence about what had happened that night, his inability or his refusal to say how the car went into the dam, was throwing everyone around him into a state of agitation that was hard to bear. … We, his fellow citizens, could not live in such a cloud of unknowing. The central fact of the matter would not let us rest. It tore at our hearts that inside the plunging car, while their father fled, three little boys had fought with their restraints, breathed filthy water, choked, thrashed and died. There was something frantic about the way we danced attendance on the silent man, this 'horrendous snorer', this 'sook', this 'good mate' and 'loving dad' and 'good provider'; this stump of a man with his low brow and puffy eyes, his slumped spine and man-boobs, his silent-movie grimaces and spasms of tears, his big clean ironed handkerchief. (ibid: 287-288) At that moment I would have given anything to be convinced that he was innocent – and not because I 'believed in him', whatever that meant, but because, in spite of everything I had heard and observed and thought in this court, in spite of everything I knew about the ways of the world, it was completely unendurable to me that a man would murder his own children. (ibid: 290)

– Questions of self and society – Ambiguities and complexities – Querying guilt, justice, and truth – Demystifying perpetrators – Racial, social and cultural diversity Hooper seeks a framework for understanding white policing in Aboriginal communities. She interrogates the Island's explosive racial and cultural fault lines from a position of familiarity and fluency – the Western literary canon – a knowledge framework the author immediately questions. – Ambiguities and complexities – Demystifying perpetrators – Racial, social and cultural diversity In tracking the lives and fates of the two men, in trying to comprehend the death of one from the actions of the other, Hooper shows the impossibility of reconciling their experiences in a society built on racism and inequality.	**HOOPER:** *The tall man* Why would a police officer choose to work solely in these communities? … For someone who feels like an outsider in the mainstream, or undervalued, or unsuccessful, or overlooked, these can be good places. Places every Mr Kurtz can go and stockpile ivory. Cops in these communities have a lot of power. … What I didn't ask the Inspector was this: Can you step into this dysfunction and desperation and not be corrupted in some way? In a community of extreme violence, are you too forced to be violent? If you are despised, as the police are, might you not feel the need to be despicable sometimes? Could anyone not be overcome by 'the growing regrets, the long to escape, the powerless disgust, the surrender, the hate'? Or had I read *Heart of darkness* too many times? (Hooper 2008: 72) What had Chris Hurley dreamt of being? What had Cameron Doomadgee? When Hurley was doing rugby training at a Christian Brothers school, Doomadgee was in a youth detention centre. By the time Hurley was setting up a sports club for the kids on Thursday Island, Cameron had a child and a broken relationship. As Hurley picked his way along the police career path, the other man was like his shadow. The date of their meeting was gaining on him. Hurley had success in his name, Cameron had doom in his. But the bitter joke of reconciliation in Australia was that the lives of these two men were supposed to be weigh equally. (ibid: 193-194)
– Intimacy and subjectivity – Questions of self and society ('whydunit') – Ambiguities and complexities – Querying guilt and truth – No (neat) endings – Demystifying perpetrators In a section titled 'Coda', Hooper's years' long struggle for understanding is over and her journalist's drive for answers disbanded. This subjective inquiry into *why* closes without insight – the mind and motives of the arsonist unknown and unknowable.	**HOOPER:** *The arsonist* Maybe, that morning, Brendan woke up inside this house and before long a dark idea took root. And maybe, by the middle of the scorching day, as he stood watching a fire truck arriving to extinguish a grassfire (the blaring siren, the flashing lights, the uniformed volunteers – a scene from the children's shows he adored, a tableau of power, adrenaline, control) the idea had grown. If he set a fire near this place where he felt inept and invisible, he could barely fight it, or warn others they were in danger. He could punish all those bad people who thought he was an idiot and be their saviour. … And there I'd go, imagining there was a reason for an act that's senseless. … I now know there isn't a standardised Arsonist. There isn't a distinct part of the brain marked by a flame. There is only the person who feels spiteful, or lonely, or anxious, or enraged, or bored, or humiliated: all the things that can set a mind – any mind – on fire. (ibid: 162)

Ruth C. Fogarty

- Victims and survivors
- Intimacy and subjectivity
- Questions of self and society
- Doubts and fears
- Ambiguities and complexities
- Querying guilt, justice and truth
- No (neat) endings
- Demystifying perpetrators
- Moral and ethical implications

Wild deploys an astonishing level of self-scrutiny throughout her investigation. Here she candidly reveals her fears and anxieties, framing her narrative engagement with Elijah's story through a highly subjective lens. There is also a rigorous and persistent ethical interrogation into the meaning of guilt, truth and justice, as well as an exploration of the writer's role and responsibility as the storyteller. Finally, Wild delivers no black and white endings, only shifts in empathy and understanding, and an acceptance of the grey zone.

WILD: *Waiting for Elijah*

Faced with the end point of my argument, my rage collapsed. I didn't want Rich to go to jail. I didn't want him punished. I wanted him not to have killed Elijah, and if I couldn't have that, I wanted Elijah's death not to be Elijah's fault. I knew I was on dangerous ground. Whoever spoke controlled the narrative. ... Stories mattered, and if you got them wrong, they mattered even more. The human brain was designed to seek out narratives or make them up to make meaning of the world. If Rich did not fill the gap in my understanding, then conjecture, assumptions, and other people's versions would flourish in the opening. I wanted to understand more than anything what drove the most difficult decision in Rich's life. (Wild 2018: 211)

Why did the compassion I felt for Elijah not flood me for Rich in his illness too? ... Even if his decision to shoot was justified, Rich could no longer explain it to us. I should have felt sorry for the damage he had suffered, but all I felt was anger. (ibid: 293)

For the last six years, I had invested police with magical powers they didn't have. The trite realisation that they were just people in uniforms dawned in every scenario I watched. I had presumed police were equipped for whatever we asked of them – that's why they had the job, because they knew what to do when no one else did. But ... they were as self-conscious and tentative about exposing themselves to another human being as I was. (ibid: 388)

Conclusion

A definition of empathy in its simplest form is to imagine ourselves in another's shoes (Joseph 2016: 211).

As a creative methodology, abiding by any rigid list of writing techniques is not viable, or even desirable, for many writers of true crime, nor do the texts cited in this case study exemplify every one of them. But as a body of work, these Australian nonfiction crime narratives demonstrate how an empathetic framework can be used to convey the complexities and lasting effects of crime, trauma and violence beyond the forensic and legal processes. In essence, these stories compel us to imagine ourselves in somebody else's shoes. Moreover, by recognising such a framework the conscientious consumer is offered a way to ethically engage with, and critically reflect upon, true crime storytelling on all platforms. By meaningfully reimagining and rearticulating the genre, these writers demonstrate the crucial role women play in facilitating public understandings of and uses for true crime, and in shaping the cultural discourse that surrounds it.

References

Adams, Phillip (director) (2004) Joe Cinque is dead, *ABC Radio National*, 23 September. Available online at https://www.abc.net.au/radionational/programs/latenightlive/joe-cinque-is-dead/3426180

Boling, Kelli S. and Hull, Kevin (2018) Undisclosed information: Serial is my favorite murder: Examining motivations in the true crime podcast audience, *Journal of Radio & Audio Media*, Vol 25, No. 1 pp 92-108. Available online at https://doi.org/10.1080/19376529.2017.1370714

Brennan, Bernadette (2017) *A writing life: Helen Garner and her work*, Text. Available online at https://www.textpublishing.com.au/books/a-writing-life-helen-garner-and-her-work

Brennan, Teresa (2004) *The transmission of affect*, Ithaca, NY, Cornell University Press. Available online at http://ebookcentral.proquest.com/lib/rmit/detail.action?docID=3138638

Eggins, Suzanne (2005) Real stories: Ethics and narrative in Helen Garner's *Joe Cinque's consolation*, *Southerly*, Vol 65, No. 1 pp 122-132. Available online at https://doi.org/10.3316/informit.433528637688426

Fitzgerald, Michael (2004) Everything but the truth: Helen Garner's attempt to shine light onto an Australian murder leaves readers in the dark, *Time International, South Pacific edition*, Vol. 32, 16 August. Available online at https://www.proquest.com/docview/214494542/3C9AC30FECA7493CPQ/1

Frow, John (2014) *Genre*, London, Taylor & Francis Group

Garner, Helen (1997) The art of the dumb question: Forethought and hindthought about *The first stone*. *LiNQ (Literature in North Queensland)*, Vol. 24, No. 2 Article 2

Garner, Helen (2002) I, *Meanjin*, 23 April. Available online at https://meanjin.com.au/essays/i/

Garner, Helen (2004) *Joe Cinque's consolation*, Sydney, Pan Macmillan AU

Garner, Helen (2014) *This house of grief: The story of a murder trial*, Melbourne, Text Publishing

Garner, Helen (2015) The darkness in every one of us, *The Monthly*, July. Available online at https://www.themonthly.com.au/issue/2015/july/1435672800/helen-garner/darkness-every-one-us

Gornick, Vivian (2002) *The situation and the story*, New York, Macmillan US

Hooper, Chloe (2008) *The tall man: Death and life on Palm Island*, Sydney, Penguin Random House Australia

Hooper, Chloe (2020) *The arsonist: A mind on fire*, Melbourne, Seven Stories Press

Horeck, Tanya (2019) *Justice on demand: True crime in the digital streaming era*, Detroit, Wayne State University Press

Joseph, Sue (2016) The empathetic profiler and ethics: Trauma narrative as advocacy, Joseph, S. and Keeble, R. L. (eds) *Profile pieces*, Abingdon, Oxon, Routledge pp 211-226

Maher, JaneMaree, McCulloch, Jude and Pickering, Sharon (2004) [W]here women face the judgement of their sisters: Review of Helen Garner (2004) *Joe Cinque's consolation, Sydney Review Essays: Current Issues in Criminal Justice*, Vol. 16, No. 2 pp 233-240

Murley, Jean (2008) *The rise of true crime: 20th-century murder and American popular culture*, Connecticut, Praeger ABC-CLIO

Murley, Jean (2017) Making murderers: The evolution of true crime, Raczkowski, C. (ed.) *A history of American crime fiction*, Cambridge, Cambridge University Press pp 288-299

Punnett, Ian Case (2018) *Toward a theory of true crime narratives: A textual analysis*, London, Taylor & Francis

Robinson, Lilian S. (1983) Treason our text: Feminist challenges to the literary canon, *Tulsa Studies in Women's Literature*, Vol. 2, No. 1 pp 83-98. Available online at https://doi.org/10.2307/464208

Rossmanith, Kate (2014) Plots and artefacts: Courts and criminal evidence in the production of true crime writing, *Australian Feminist Law Journal*, Vol. 40, No. 1 pp 97-111. Available online at https://doi.org/10.1080/13200968.2014.931903

Shute, Carmel (2018) The long wait for justice: Q&A with Kate Wild, *Sisters in Crime Australia* blog, 15 October. Available online at https://sistersincrime.org.au/the-long-wait-for-justice-qa-with-kate-wild/

Smith, Rosalind (2008) Dark places: True crime writing in Australia, *Journal of the Association for the Study of Australian Literature*, Vol. 8 pp 17-30. Available online at https://openjournals.library.sydney.edu.au/index.php/JASAL/article/view/9731

Telfer, Tori (2019) True crime advice: Is the 'true crime boom' a real thing?, *CrimeReads*, 27 February. Available online at https://crimereads.com/true-crime-advice-is-the-true-crime-boom-a-real-thing/

Vicary, Amanda M. and Fraley, R. Chris (2010) Captured by true crime: Why are women drawn to tales of rape, murder, and serial killers?, *Social Psychological and Personality Science*, Vol. 1, No. 1 pp 81-86. Available online at https://doi.org/10.1177/1948550609355486

Weinman, Sarah (2020) True crime has been having a moment for three centuries. But the new era is different, *CrimeReads*, 28 July. Available online at https://crimereads.com/true-crime-has-been-having-a-moment-for-three-centuries-but-the-new-era-is-different/

Wild, Kate (2018) *Waiting for Elijah*, Melbourne, Scribe Publications

Wright, Hazel (2020) *Ethics and true crime: Setting a standard for the genre*, Portland State University. Available online at https://pdxscholar.library.pdx.edu/eng_bookpubpaper/51/

Note on the contributor

Ruth C. Fogarty is a PhD researcher at the Royal Melbourne Institute of Technology, exploring perceptions and potentialities of the true crime genre, through podcasting, digital storytelling and literary nonfiction. She is an award-winning digital journalist with a professional background in current affairs broadcasting. She advises on and teaches digital and social media strategies for the tertiary education sector, government, public broadcasting, non-profits, arts and cultural institutions.

Conflict of interest

The author is not funded for her PhD research, nor did she receive any financial aid to research, write or publish this paper.

PAPER

Lili Pâquet

A police-run true crime podcast: A comparison of justice in *State crime command – investigations*, *Bowraville* and *Phoebe's fall*

In 2020, the police force of New South Wales, Australia, began to distribute a true crime podcast titled State crime command – investigations. *My previous research investigates the attempts of true crime podcasts to fill 'justice gaps' in formal institutions such as police and courts. By addressing these justice gaps, the true crime podcasts act as mediums of informal justice – forms of reparation outside those formal systems – particularly for victim-survivors and secondary victims of gender-based violence. In this paper, I evaluate* State crime command – investigations *for its attempts to address justice gaps through a comparison with two well-known Australian podcasts,* Phoebe's fall *(2016) and* Bowraville *(2016). The paper concludes that the police true crime podcast seeks information from listeners without attempting to fill any justice gaps and, therefore, seems more useful as an advertisement of investigative procedure, a recruitment strategy, or a tool for tying up the loose ends of investigations.*

Keywords: justice, feminism, true crime, podcast, Australian

Introduction
True crime podcasts overlap formal and informal justice, with podcasts and investigations informing and transforming each other. Previous research on true crime podcasts as sites of informal justice that work outside formal systems concludes that police could tap into community grapevines through the genre (Pâquet 2021). Here, this idea is tested using the case study of a police-initiated true crime podcast, *State crime command – investigations* (*SCC*). The podcast was created by the New South Wales police about cold cases. Launched in late 2020, it includes interviews with witnesses and personal anecdotes from detectives as they appeal to the public for aid. My research evaluates how the police have adapted the potential community outreach of the true crime genre and medium, further blurring the boundaries between formal and informal justice. I compare the podcast to two well-received Australian podcasts: *Bowraville* (2016) and *Phoebe's fall* (2016).

Phoebe's fall is narrated by investigative journalists Richard Baker and Michael Bachelard, of *The Age* newspaper. Throughout six episodes, Baker and Bachelard investigate the mysterious death of twenty-four-year-old Phoebe Handsjuk, who fell feet first down her Melbourne apartment building's garbage chute and died of injuries inflicted by the compactor. The coroner ruled her death a suicide, while Handsjuk's family has always been suspicious of her boyfriend, Ant Hampel.

Throughout five episodes narrated by Dan Box of *The Australian* newspaper, *Bowraville* investigates the largely ignored and unsolved serial killings of three First Nations children in the regional town of Bowraville, in 1990 and 1991. Sixteen-year-old Colleen Walker-Craig, four-year-old Evelyn Greenup and sixteen-year-old Clinton Speedy-Duroux all disappeared from house parties in the same area of Bowraville known, because of historical segregation, as The Mission. The podcast highlights racial inequalities in Australia's justice system.

In these podcasts, the narrators incorporate the creative techniques of true crime — a genre that plays with narration, characterisation and setting — to foster audience interest. How can a formal criminal justice institution adapt the genre and medium to solve cold cases? Is it as effective as true crime podcasts by journalists who are independent from formal justice institutions?

SCC has not produced the online buzz, perhaps due to the constraints listeners feel when conversing directly with police. Victim-survivors and secondary victims (ie. victims' family members) might feel some justice is achieved when they are socially connected with podcast audiences (McGlynn and Westmarland 2019). Both *Phoebe's fall* and *Bowraville* discuss police missteps in murder investigations that caused public outcry, leading to changes in formal justice.

Methodology

Since the popularity of Sarah Koenig's first season of *Serial* (2014), podcasting has become a common medium for the true crime genre. A portmanteau of 'portable' and 'broadcast' developed in 2004, podcasts are digital audio stories streamed through a listener's smartphone at a time and place that suits them (McClung and Johnson 2010: 83). Australia has high podcast consumption (Newman 2018: 30; Riordan 2018). Following the blueprint set by *Serial*, true crime podcasts release episodes at staggered intervals, drawing out a sustained and in-depth investigation. Australian true crime podcasts have led to new inquests and arrests for historic murders, such as those following *Trace* (Brown 2017-2018) and *The teacher's pet* (Thomas 2018). I evaluate two Australian examples, *Phoebe's fall* and *Bowraville*, because these podcasts represent similar ideas of families seeking informal justice through audio storytelling. These podcasts are then compared to the police true crime podcast, *State crime command – investigations,* which attempts to tap into community sources of information to solve crime while using a medium that seems to rely on its separation from formal systems. I focus on the extended stories in *SCC* for a more reasonable comparison, namely the 'Lost at sea', 'Mary Wallace', and 'Lost at sea: The black bone' sequences.

Within my analysis, formal justice is referred to as everything that takes place within established institutional systems such as police and courts, while informal justice is referred to as all forms of reparation outside those formal systems. As I have defined it elsewhere, informal justice:

> … includes a gamut of possible procedures such as Indigenous, religious, and traditional justice, through to vigilantism and slacktivism. … [It can also encompass] an approach through podcasts by creators, victim-survivors, and audiences, to seek reparation for crimes that were left unsolved by formal justice systems. (Pâquet 2021: 425)

Research suggests that true crime is a genre which, whether paperback or podcast, is largely consumed by women (Browder 2006; Vicary and Fraley 2010; Cunningham 2018; Boling and Hull 2018). The reasons for this skew in audience gender are attributed to women's fear of crime (Kort-Butler and Hartshorn 2011) and dissatisfaction with the current state of the justice system (Browder 2006). Researchers have investigated the emancipatory affordances of new media, such as podcasts, but also lament its reproduction of harmful gender dynamics (Powell 2015; Harris and Vitis 2020). As Michael Salter argues, the representation of women in media 'reflects and legitimizes the gender biases within other democratic institutions such as the criminal justice system, in which cultural mythologies around gender and sexuality have proven to be particularly durable, blunting the impacts of feminist-inspired law reform' (Salter 2013: 226-227). According to Fileborn (2017: 1484-1485), female victim-survivors feel justice is achieved when they have real participation, an active voice, vindication and a tangible outcome such as admission of guilt. These ideas problematise a police-run true crime podcast that seeks to gather information and focuses on the voices of formal justice professionals.

Phoebe's fall

Phoebe's fall opens with the discovery of Phoebe Handsjuk's body. It is given in a scene of action to draw in listeners through a sense of immediacy:

> Melbourne, Thursday 2 September 2010. At seven o'clock on this summer evening, it was still hot and muggy. At a luxury apartment building, the concierge made her way to the refuse room on the ground floor. There'd been a fire alarm and she was looking for a broom to sweep up a mess. When she turned the key, something blocked the door. She gave the door a shove. It shifted a bit and she peered in. She saw the body of a young woman lying in a pool of blood among the fallen bins. Somehow, twelve floors above, this young woman had squeezed through a narrow hatch one metre off the floor and fallen feet first forty metres down the galvanised steel chute. (Baker and Bachelard 2016b)

An important element of audio storytelling, such as true crime podcasts, is that it conveys a sense of action and is 'told by the people in it' (Carlisle 2017: 2-3). *Phoebe's fall* faced challenges in how many people would not talk to the reporters. The narrators rely instead on voice actors reading transcripts from the inquest and on re-enactments, such as Handsjuk's friends attempting to climb into garbage chute replicas (Baker and Bachelard 2016c). As Carlisle points out, the podcast is reported 'in a second or third-hand way rather than letting the characters tell their first-hand stories' (2017: 3). The lack of many first-hand accounts is obscured by aural action. Scene setting such as the example

Lili Pâquet

above is combined with background sounds of walking, doors opening and closing, car engines turning over and other ambient noise to give the story movement. *Phoebe's fall* also focuses on the process of journalism, such as the sounds of typing.

The two narrators' conversation replaces conspicuously missing stories: those of Handsjuk and her boyfriend Ant Hampel who, it is inferred, knows more about her death than he claims. Their voices are represented through audio recordings. In the first episode, listeners hear Handsjuk reading a poem at a funeral (Baker and Bachelard 2016b), and in another episode hear Hampel in a secret recording made by Handsjuk's suspicious mother (Baker and Bachelard 2016c). Much of the first episode of the podcast focuses on characterisation of Handsjuk (Baker and Bachelard 2016b) and later episodes are interspersed with her poems, giving audiences a more personalised, emotional connection to her. Hampel declines an interview for the podcast. Baker and Bachelard describe his links to the formal justice system, as the son of a retired Supreme Court judge whose sister escaped jail time for a drug-related conviction. There is a doubling effect in the story of Handsjuk's family chasing informal justice away from the courts and police, and away from the Hampel family.

The podcast focuses on mistakes in the investigation of Handsjuk's death, which lead to the coroner's finding of suicide. First responders ignored ambiguous physical evidence to focus on evidence of suicide. As the podcast narrators point out, 'It seems like from the very first, on the night she was discovered, that Phoebe and her family were let down by the system' (Baker and Bachelard 2016b). Police did not retrieve vital CCTV footage or blood evidence. Handsjuk's family later discover CCTV hardware was missing (Baker and Bachelard 2016e).

The experience left Handsjuk's family disillusioned with formal justice. Following the inquest, Handsjuk's brother says: 'There's this façade that's maintained that you're always protected, the state's there, there are all these systems in place, but really that's all rubbish.' Lawyers offer to work on an appeal pro-bono but inform the family it could cost more than $120,000 (AUD) if they are unsuccessful. Handsjuk's mother states: 'I did walk away feeling like there's not a justice system' (Baker and Bachelard 2016f). The podcast draws attention to the problems with the Victorian coronial rulings and appeals processes (Baker and Bachelard 2016a).

Bowraville

Bowraville is produced by *The Australian*, a commercial news publisher owned by Rupert Murdoch's NewsCorp, and as such the podcast — unlike *Phoebe's fall* — has pre- and mid-roll advertisements. The mid-roll advertisements intrude on the intimacy of the narrative created through the narrator's voice (Dowling and Miller 2019, 171). Podcasts are increasingly produced by commercial Australian media. As Carlisle suggests: 'Digital technology has democratised the audio storytelling space in a quite profound way. Established radio media, primarily the *ABC* and *SBS*, no longer have a mortgage on the audio space in Australia' (2017: 13). The murders of three First Nations children in Bowraville was largely neglected by Australian media and audiences until the narrator brought it to wider scrutiny. Dan Box uses the medium of the podcast to investigate the murders with sensitivity, giving families a chance to express their pain and sense of injustice in their own voices.

The opening credits of *Bowraville* have repetition of different people saying they want 'justice'. The first episode outlines a timeline of the murders and investigations. All victims are described as last seen near a white neighbour called Jay Hart, and each is linked to the sexual harassment or assault of a woman. Police told family members the victims had probably 'gone walkabout'. Box uses setting to highlight the racial elements of the investigations:

> This part of town is called The Mission, and to understand what happened to the children you need to know a little bit about Bowraville itself ... The town is segregated by race. At the time the children disappeared, Bowraville had about 1,100 people, maybe 350 of them Aboriginal. And it felt like two towns. There was the white town on top of the hill and there was The Mission, which was built between the town's cemetery, piggery, and rubbish tip. (Box 2016a)

Within this setting, First Nations inhabitants of Bowraville felt unsupported by the police. Box interviews numerous First Nations people including Hart's ex-girlfriend and mother of his child, Alison Walker, who describes her experiences of domestic abuse, and how police never charged Hart. A First Nations man describes how Hart confessed to the killings to him, but does not make a statement to police because he distrusts them (Box 2016c). While *Phoebe's fall* provides aural cues of action to give the story momentum, *Bowraville* centres on setting and characterisation through interviews. The sense of place established in the first episode aids Box in communicating the racial injustices that characterise the murder investigation.

Contrary to legitimate concerns that secondary victims may not have 'ownership of their loss' (Yardley et al. 2017: 472), in *Bowraville* they feature prominently; Box interviews seventeen community members. Fears that white victims have the majority of access to informal and formal justice (Serisier 2018; Webb 2021), and that true crime podcasts do not investigate the social construction of gender-based violence (Slakoff 2022) are both challenged by and asserted within *Bowraville*. The podcast provides a voice to non-white victims of crime but also questions Australians' ignorance of the crimes until its distribution. Gary Jubelin, the detective who led a strike force re-investigation of the murders, tells Box:

> When three children living in the same street are murdered over a five-month period, and the justice system can't bring the person accountable for that to justice, I think the justice system has let them down. (Box 2016b)

He has started to agree over his twenty years on the case that Australians have not cared because the victims were First Nations' children. Judicial decisions and legalities mean that Hart has never faced a trial for all three murders at once. Hart was acquitted of Speedy-Duroux's murder in 1994, and Greenup's murder in 2006. In 2016 changes to double jeopardy legislation in New South Wales meant that a person could face retrial for a crime they were acquitted of if there were fresh and compelling new evidence (NSW Legislative Assembly 2016). A subsequent application for a retrial was dismissed (Attorney General for NSW vs XX 2018). Hart's identity was under a suppression order from 2017 to protect him against bias in any potential trials, but after the High Court's 2019 decision, documentary-makers argued for the lifting of the suppression order and were successful in 2020. *Bowraville* concludes by questioning the difficulty of navigating the formal system and the racism inherent in these investigations.

State crime command – investigations

The three stories given extended serialised airtime in *SCC* are 'Lost at sea', which follows police attempts to identify remains that washed up on NSW's Kingscliff Beach in 2011; 'Case: Mary Wallace', about the protracted investigation of a murder with a known suspect; and 'Lost at sea: The black bone' about an ongoing investigation into unidentified remains washed up on NSW'S Umina Beach. Other episodes are sporadic stand-alone stories of missing persons.

True crime podcasts produced by the media have differences in their presentation of justice to that in *SCC*. Formal justice systems define conviction as justice and the victim is hardly ever in a position to define their own sense of justice (McGlynn and Westmarland 2019: 180-181). Both *Phoebe's fall* and *Bowraville* infer instances of gender-based violence, in which no conviction was attained. Australian legal responses to domestic abuse are minimal (Easteal et al. 2018). Women's voices are lost in court trials about sexual assault (Cotterill 2003; Matoesian 1993; Quilter 2016) and there is a 'justice gap' between incidents of sexual violence and low conviction rates (Russell 2016: 276). Powell argues that women may find 'a more victim-centred approach' to justice '*outside of the state*' (2015: 573 original emphasis). The internet is a counter-public space where women might find their justice needs are met more readily than through formal systems (Fileborn 2017).

Both previous podcasts directly deal with justice gaps. *Phoebe's fall* focuses on the tragedy of Handsjuk's death, potentially through a violent encounter, and how her family feel no involvement or justice in the inquest process. As the narrators explain, in the eight years prior there was only one appeal to a coroner's finding. The podcast led to some action in changing the appeal process. The deputy leader of the Victorian National Party, Stephanie Ryan, used parliamentary privilege to call for a formal review of the coroner's finding on Handsjuk's death, and the narrators follow up the podcast with an update that explains: 'The public feedback after *Phoebe's fall* … has been overwhelming. There have been offers to set up a crowdfunding drive to fund an appeal' (Baker and Bachelard 2016a). *Bowraville* focuses on the double jeopardy legislation that means Hart could not be retried and motivated some changes in those laws (2016d).

In contrast, *SCC* focuses on investigative procedure rather than failures to produce justice. The 'Lost at sea' group of episodes opens with the narrator, Adam Shand, describing how part of a jawbone washed ashore on Kingscliff Beach. It was unidentified until 2020, when DNA technology advanced enough to find a familial match. The owner of the jawbone died in a boating accident decades earlier. As the police interviewee blandly explains, 'by following that trail it did lead to a result' (Shand 2021c). The interviews with police and specialists are often delivered in stilted monotone. The 'Lost at sea' story is solved in one episode, and then two more episodes detail the boating accident. The story loses its urgency; the only villain is nature. The podcast often focuses on investigative procedure rather than the criminal story that captures listener attention in podcasts such as *Phoebe's fall* and *Bowraville*. Despite those two podcasts investigating historical crimes, the narrators set up urgency through justice gaps, told compellingly by secondary victims.

This point leads to another difference in the podcasts: the lack of emotion in *SCC*. According to Sara Ahmed in *The cultural politics of emotions*, fear is used by writers to connect women readers through their own bodily fear of violence (2014: 70). This empathic connection can align female audiences with the women they read about against 'characters' who incite violence (ibid: 72). The victim-survivors or secondary victims represented by podcasts can feel a sense of justice through connection with empathic audiences (McGlynn and Westmarland 2019: 194). These victim-survivors must also be able to participate in voicing their experiences (2019: 192). Speaking out offers a change to social perceptions and representations of sexual violence rather than only focusing on legal changes (Serisier 2018: 54). In *SCC*, the three episodes that encompass 'Case: Mary Wallace' include these elements of a compelling true crime story. It focuses on the murder of Mary Wallace by a known suspect, and the difficulty faced by detectives due to the lack of a body or evidence. However, the first episode (Shand 2021a) explains that the murderer is in prison for the crime, immediately foreclosing any sense of urgency.

Unlike a formal system that seeks justice through conviction, true crime podcasts often resist a sense of closure. The cold cases investigated in the podcasts allow narrators and listeners to share information in order to achieve mutual realisations about justice. Podcasts are 'neither celebratory of the criminal justice system nor conclusive' (Yardley et al. 2019: 511). As Bruzzi suggests, 'part of this genre's dynamism is that it remains resistant to closure, seeking instead to keep its cases alive and open' (2016: 278). Podcasts breathe new life into cold cases, attempting to give families a sense of informal justice through a more community-driven and less institutional process.

Three episodes in *SCC* that have no sense of closure are 'Lost at sea: The black bone', following an investigation into a jawbone washed up on Umina Beach. It is confirmed as recent remains from a teenager or young man. At its beginning, Shand says: 'Police are reviewing all the evidence in this case and they need your help. If something in this podcast sparks a memory or even a thought, make sure you share it with police or call Crimestoppers' (2021d). The episodes proceed to detail tediously the investigative procedure with no closure. As a true crime narrative, a long and inconclusive identification of a body is not a compelling or satisfying story.

SCC asks for information from its listeners, whereas *Phoebe's fall* and *Bowraville* invite judgements. In the final episode of *Bowraville*, this invitation is explicit: 'How strong is the case that [Hart] is innocent? This time you be the judge' (Box 2016d). Box then has a phone conversation with Hart, allowing him an opportunity to explain his perspective. *Phoebe's fall* examines evidence that potentially implicates Hampel, without ever explicitly communicating blame, leaving it to the judgement of listeners. The podcasters also do not have the opportunity to provide Hampel's perspective on Handsjuk's death beyond a secret recording made of a conversation he had with Handsjuk's mother. By inviting listeners to make judgements, the narrators provide 'a mass media version of these women-centred counter-publics. They invite listeners to look back at the historical justice gap … and rectify it informally [and] socially' (Pâquet 2021: 429).

An interesting section of *SCC*'s 'Case: Mary Wallace' episodes explains that because the murderer decided to represent himself in court, he was able to cross-examine witnesses directly (Shand 2021b). Rather than focusing on this justice gap for women facing their abusers in the formal system, Shand moves the story along. As a police-initiated podcast, it is clear the narrator does not have the freedom to make judgements on the inadequacies of the system. This lack of freedom does not lend itself to a true crime podcast, many of which act 'as a double-check for the performance of law enforcement' (Punnett 2018: 106) and produce positive changes.

Conclusion

This paper set out to answer two questions through a comparison of the Australian true crime podcasts *Phoebe's fall*, *Bowraville*, and *State crime command – investigations*. Firstly, how can a formal criminal justice institution adapt the genre and medium of true crime podcasts to solve cold cases? *SCC* attempts to draw audiences into cold cases by lifting the curtain, so to speak, on the investigative procedure and the professionals who undertake formal investigations. Adam Shand is an experienced journalist who uses descriptive passages and compelling inflection. He is, however, hamstrung by the necessity of interviewing professionals about their work, meaning that while they can show empathy and compassion in unsolved cases, they cannot criticise the system they represent. In the other true crime podcasts, criticism overwhelmingly comes from those outside the formal system, such as secondary victims and retired professionals. The cases discussed in *SCC* are often solved, and police are seeking information to find or identify remains. While important work, this information-seeking does not necessarily provide foundations for a long-form, serialised format. The focus on investigative procedure without a more compelling and urgent story is difficult to sustain; it sounds more like a recruitment strategy than a call for urgent information. At the same time, the attempt of police to use the form and medium of true crime podcasts — an increasingly popular genre — to solve cold cases is commendable.

Secondly, is *SCC* as effective as podcasts by journalists who are independent from formal justice institutions? True crime podcasts are open-ended, inviting listeners to connect emotionally with the victims of crime represented and to make their own judgements on guilt or innocence. Formal justice institutions define justice on convictions, whereas informal justice might instead focus more on the feelings of victims and secondary victims: that they have their voices heard and validated; are accepted by a community of peers; and have had acceptance of guilt by the person who wronged them. It is a more nuanced idea of justice that depends on the victim more than a necessarily rigid system. When narrators include victim-survivors and secondary victims in the creation of a true crime podcast, informal justice can be obtained. In some cases, the outcry in the supportive community of readers leads to changes to formal systems. To make these changes, the narrator(s) must be working from outside the system, within counter-publics, and have freedom to criticise justice gaps in order to have them resolved. In both *Phoebe's fall* and *Bowraville*, the secondary victims have felt ignored and disenfranchised by police, coroners and courts. Through the podcasts they have had their stories heard and validated by communities of listeners and this has led to changes in formal justice systems that they have not achieved on their own. Perhaps by working, whether implicitly or explicitly, with external true crime podcasters, police and courts would better achieve a sense of justice for victims.

References

Ahmed, Sara (2014) *The cultural politics of emotions*, Edinburgh, Edinburgh University Press

Attorney General for New South Wales v XX (2018), NSWCCA 198. Available online at https://www.caselaw.nsw.gov.au/decision/5b971f9be4b06629b6c61ca1, accessed on 24 May 2022

Baker, Richard and Bachelard, Michael (2016a) Bonus: Phoebe's fall, a fresh look, *Phoebe's fall* [Podcast], *The Age*, 15 December. Available online at https://www.smh.com.au/interactive/2016/phoebesfall/index.html, accessed on 24 May 2022

Baker, Richard and Bachelard, Michael (2016b) Episode 1: Knowing Phoebe, *Phoebe's fall* [Podcast], *The Age*, 22 September. Available online at https://www.smh.com.au/interactive/2016/phoebesfall/index.html, accessed on 24 May 2022

Baker, Richard and Bachelard, Michael (2016c) Episode 2: The chute, *Phoebe's fall* [Podcast], *The Age*, 28 September. Available online at https://www.smh.com.au/interactive/2016/phoebesfall/index.html, accessed on 24 May 2022

Baker, Richard and Bachelard, Michael (2016d) Episode 3: A secret tape, *Phoebe's fall* [Podcast], *The Age*, 6 October. Available online at https://www.smh.com.au/interactive/2016/phoebesfall/index.html, accessed on 24 May 2022

Baker, Richard and Bachelard, Michael (2016e) Episode 4: Policework, *Phoebe's fall* [Podcast], *The Age*, 13 October. Available online at https://www.smh.com.au/interactive/2016/phoebesfall/index.html, accessed on 24 May 2022

Baker, Richard and Bachelard, Michael (2016f) Episode 6: Inquest & aftermath, *Phoebe's fall* [Podcast], *The Age*, 27 October. Available online at https://www.smh.com.au/interactive/2016/phoebesfall/index.html, accessed on 24 May 2022

Boling, Kelli S. and Hull, Kevin (2018) Undisclosed information – *Serial* is my favourite murder: Examining motivation in the true crime podcast audience, *Journal of Radio and Audio Media*, Vol. 25, No. 1 pp 92-108

Box, Dan (2016a) Episode 1: The murders, *Bowraville* [Podcast], *The Australian*, 4 May. Available online at https://www.theaustralian.com.au/nation/bowraville-episode-1-the-murders/audio/40c218571c651374014400b8b246443e, accessed on 24 May 2022

Box, Dan (2016b) Episode 2: The investigation, *Bowraville* [Podcast], *The Australian*, 8 May. Available online at https://www.theaustralian.com.au/nation/bowraville-episode-2-the-investigation/audio/564cc160e7b523ab362c5a330ea65cef, accessed on 24 May 2022

Box, Dan (2016c) Episode 3: The suspect, *Bowraville* [Podcast], *The Australian*, 11 May. Available online at https://www.theaustralian.com.au/nation/bowraville-episode-3-the-suspect/audio/f4367f87489ac5b46312b7dbae2c5c47, accessed on 24 May 2022

Box, Dan (2016d) Episode 5: The case for Jay, *Bowraville* [Podcast], *The Australian*, 18 May. Available online at https://www.theaustralian.com.au/nation/bowraville-episode-5-the-case-for-jay/audio/7be5e5408532bfb5d663e6424c41b79e, accessed on 24 May 2022

Browder, Laura (2006) Dystopian romance: True crime and the female reader, *The Journal of Popular Culture*, Vol. 39, No. 6 pp 928-953

Brown, Rachael (2017-2018) Trace [Podcast], *ABC*. Available online at https://www.abc.net.au/radio/programs/trace/season-1/12490438, accessed on 8 December 2018

Bruzzi, Stella (2016) Making a genre: The case of the contemporary true crime documentary, *Law and Humanities*, Vol. 10, No. 2 pp 249-280

Lili Pâquet

Carlisle, Wendy (2017) *Bowraville* and *Phoebe's fall*: Award-winning Australian podcasts from the media formerly known as print, *RadioDoc Review*, Vol. 3, No. 2

Cotterill, Janet (2003) *Language and power in court: A linguistic analysis of the O.J. Simpson trial*, Basingstoke, Palgrave Macmillan

Cunningham, Katie (2018) Women are fuelling the growth of true crime podcasts. Here's why, *ABC*, 18 December. Available online at www.abc.net.au/life/why-women-love-true-crime-podcasts/10627390, accessed on 13 June 2019

Dowling, David O. and Miller, Kyle J. (2019) Immersive audio storytelling: Podcasting and serial documentary in the digital publishing industry, *Journal of Radio & Audio Media*, Vol. 26, No. 1 pp 167-184

Easteal, Patricia, Young, Lisa and Carline, Anna (2018) Domestic violence, property and family law in Australia, *International Journal of Law, Policy and The Family*, Vol. 32, No. 2 pp 204–229

Fileborn, Bianca (2017) Justice 2.0: Street harassment victims' use of social media and online activism as sites of informal justice, *British Journal of Criminology*, Vol. 57 pp 1482–1501

Harris, Bridget and Vitis, Laura (2020) Digital intrusions: Technology, spatiality and violence against women, *Journal of Gender-Based Violence*, Vol. 4, No. 3 pp 325-341

Koenig, Sarah (2014) *Serial* [Podcast], *The New York Times*. Available online at https://serialpodcast.org/season-one

Kort-Butler, Lisa A. and Hartshorn, Kelley J. Sittner (2011) Watching the detectives: Crime programming, fear of crime, and attitudes about the criminal justice system, *Sociological Quarterly*, Vol. 52, No. 1 pp 36-55

Matoesian, Gregory M. (1993) *Reproducing rape domination through talk in the courtroom*, Cambridge, Polity Press

McClung, Steven and Johnson, Kristine (2010) Examining the motives of podcast users, *Journal of Radio & Audio Media*, Vol. 17. No. 1 pp 82-95

McGlynn, Clare and Westmarland, Nicole (2019) Kaleidoscopic justice: Sexual violence and victim-survivors' perceptions of justice, *Social & Legal Studies*, Vol. 28, No. 2, pp 179-201

Newman, Nic, Fletcher, Richard, Kalogeropoulos, Antonis et al. (2018) Reuters Institute digital news report, *Reuters Institute for the Study of Journalism*. Available online at https://reutersinstitute.politics.ox.ac.uk/sites/default/files/digital-news-report-2018.pdf, accessed on 24 May 2022

NSW Legislative Assembly, Crimes (appeals and review) amendment (double jeopardy) bill (2006). Available online at https://www.parliament.nsw.gov.au/bills/Pages/Profiles/crimes-appeal-and-review-amendment-double-jeopar_1.aspx, accessed on 24 May 2022

Pâquet, Lili (2021) Seeking justice elsewhere: Informal and formal justice in the true crime podcasts *Trace* and *The teacher's pet*, *Crime Media Culture*, Vol. 17, No. 3 pp 421-437

Powell, Anastasia (2015) Seeking rape justice: Formal and informal responses to sexual violence through technosocial counter-publics, *Theoretical Criminology*, Vol. 19, No. 4 pp 571-588

Punnett, Ian Case (2018) *Toward a theory of true crime narratives: A textual analysis*, New York and London, Routledge

Quilter, Julia (2016) Rape trials, medical texts and the threat of female speech: The perverse female rape complainant, *Law Text Culture*, Vol. 19 pp 231-270

Riordan, Kelly (2018) Commentary: The mobile phone as the new transistor radio, Park, Sora, Fisher, Caroline, Fuller, Glen, et al. (eds) *Digital news report: Australia* [Report], News and Media Research Centre, University of Canberra

Russell, Yvette (2016) Woman's voice/law's *logos*: The rape trial and the limits of liberal reform, *Australian Feminist Law Journal*, Vol. 42, No. 2 pp 273-296

Salter, Michael (2013) Justice and revenge in online counter-publics: Emerging responses to sexual violence in the age of social media, *Crime, Media, Culture: An International Journal*, Vol. 9, No. 3 pp 225-242

Serisier, Tanya (2018) Speaking out, and beginning to be heard: Feminism, survivor narratives and representations of rape in the 1980s, *Continuum: Journal of Media & Cultural Studies*, Vol. 32, No. 1 pp 52-61

Shand, Adam (2021a) Case: Mary Wallace, Episode 1: justice for Mary, *State crime command – investigations* [Podcast], The NSW Police Force, 7 July. Available online at https://www.police.nsw.gov.au/safety_and_prevention/policing_in_the_community/podcast, accessed on 24 May 2022

Shand, Adam (2021b) Case: Mary Wallace, Episode 2: building a case, *State crime command – investigations* [Podcast], The NSW Police Force, 7 July. Available online at https://www.police.nsw.gov.au/safety_and_prevention/policing_in_the_community/podcast, accessed on 24 May 2022

Shand, Adam (2021c) Case: Lost at sea, Episode 1: Kingscliff, *State crime command – investigations* [Podcast], The NSW Police Force, 6 February. Available online at https://www.police.nsw.gov.au/safety_and_prevention/policing_in_the_community/podcast, accessed on 24 May 2022

Shand, Adam (2021d) Lost at sea: The black bone, part 1, *State crime command – investigations* [Podcast], The NSW Police Force, 13 December. Available online at https://www.police.nsw.gov.au/safety_and_prevention/policing_in_the_community/podcast, accessed on 24 May 2022

Slakoff, Danielle C. (2022) The mediated portrayal of intimate partner violence in true crime podcasts: Strangulation, isolation, threats of violence, and coercive control, *Violence Against Women*, Vol. 28, No. 6-7 pp 1659-1683

Thomas, Hedley (2018) *The teacher's pet* [Podcast], *The Australian*. Available online at https://podcasts.apple.com/au/podcast/the-teachers-pet/id1385379989, accessed on 5 December 2018

Vicary, Amanda M. and Fraley, R. Chris (2010) Captured by true crime: Why are women drawn to tales of rape, murder, and serial killers? *Social Psychological and Personality Science*, Vol. 1, No. 1 pp 81-86

Webb, Lindsey (2021) True crime and danger narratives: Reflections on stories of violence, race and (in)justice, *Journal of Gender, Race & Justice*, Vol. 131 pp 131-170

Yardley, Elizabeth, Kelly, Emma and Robinson-Edwards, Shona (2019) Forever trapped in the imaginary of late capitalism? The serialized true crime podcast as a wake-up call in times of criminological slumber, *Crime, Media, Culture: An International Journal*, Vol. 15, No. 3 pp 503-521

Yardley, Elizabeth, Wilson, David and Kennedy, Morag (2017) 'To me its [sic] real life': Secondary victims of homicide in newer media, *Victims and Offenders: An International Journal of Evidence-Based Research, Policy, and Practice*, Vol. 12, No. 3 pp 467-496

Note on the contributor

Lili Pâquet is a Lecturer in Writing at the University of New England, Australia, with research interests in rhetoric, crime, environmental humanities and digital media. Her book is titled *Crime fiction from a professional eye: Women writers with law enforcement and Justice experience* (2018) and she is published in journals including *Crime, Media, Culture*, *Computers and Composition*, *Rhetoric Society Quarterly* and *New Writing*.

Conflict of interest

No funding was received for this research.

PAPER

George S. Larke-Walsh

The ethics of bearing witness: Subject empowerment versus true crime intrigue in Kim Longinotto's *Shooting the mafia* (2019)

The ethics of bearing witness to testimony on true crime events is affected by the way a documentary chooses to frame it and the way it is contextualised within the larger narrative of events. To create empathy, films must detail the danger and horrors witnessed, but this risks framing testimony within victimhood. Topics of violent crime, especially on the scale of the Sicilian mafia, encourage audience expectations of sensation and intrigue. These expectations are influenced by the conventions and popularity of the true crime genre which threaten to drown out individual testimony and reduce films to intriguing exposé of mafia secrets. This paper explores Kim Longinotto's Shooting the mafia *(2019) as an ethical practice that avoids such pitfalls and thus empowers its subject to challenge true crime conventions.*

Keywords: ethics, documentary, mafia, *verité*, empowerment, Kim Longinotto

Introduction

In previously published work I discuss the ways Kim Longinotto's documentary filmmaking style 'displays her passionate involvement while simultaneously downplaying her presence' (Larke-Walsh 2019: 148) and encourages audiences to bear witness to the testimony of her subjects. Longinotto's recent documentary *Shooting the mafia* (2019) continues this tradition through interviews with the Sicilian photojournalist Letizia Battaglia (1935-2022) discussing her work documenting the mafia wars in Palermo during the 1970s and 1980s. Strong female subjects are prevalent in Longinotto's films and while many of her topics include crime, they tend to focus mainly on issues that affect female safety and empowerment such as domestic and/or sexual abuse.

Large-scale mafia violence is arguably a more challenging arena in which to create a portrait of female empowerment. First, in order to create empathy for Battaglia's experiences, the film must detail the danger and horrors witnessed. This approach risks framing her testimony within notions of victimhood rather than activism. Second, topics of violent crime, especially on the scale of the Sicilian mafia, encourage audience expectations of sensation and intrigue. These expectations are influenced by the conventions and popularity of the true crime genre which threaten to drown out Battaglia's testimony and turn the film into yet another intriguing exposé of mafia secrets. This paper examines the ethics of subject testimony in *Shooting the mafia* and how its specific style and focus on women's voices offer a challenge to the conventions and entertaining intrigue associated with true crime, but cannot truly undermine it.

Ethics and documentary styles

Bill Nichols (2016: 151) reminds us that unlike journalism, sociology, anthropology and other disciplines, there is 'no code of conduct, no set of ethical standards that governs all documentary filmmaking'. Similarly, Brian Winston (2005: 181) makes it clear that ethical conduct is a significant topic of debate for documentary: although its claim on 'actuality' requires that it behave ethically, its 'unjournalistic parallel desire to be allowed to be creative' permits a measure of 'artistic amorality'. Indeed, documentary has long relied on a generally accepted 'tacit agreement' between filmmaker and audience that what is shown is factual. Or as Louise Spence and Vinicius Navarro (2011: 24) write: 'Documentarians are expected to earn the trust of the audience by offering truthful information about their subjects.' Throughout the years, certain documentary styles have been credited as more ethical than others.

Since its emergence in the late 1950s, *cinéma verité* is applauded as one of the hallowed ethical filmmaking techniques (Williams 2016) due to its seeming desire to avoid the mediatisation of events. *Verité* conventions mirror the spontaneity of home videos, recording events and interviews in a casually intimate manner that foregrounds notions of authenticity and objec-

George S. Larke-Walsh

tivity. It is often applied interchangeably with another objective style of the time, direct cinema, but it is important to note that while direct cinema values non-interventionist observation, *verité* draws attention to the camera as conduit for testimony, or confession. Hence, in *verité*, audiences are aware of an interviewer, even if they are not present on screen. Therefore, the style prioritises interviews, but it avoids the formality of talking heads, and it also avoids montage or voice-over – all of the styles that may suggest forced characterisation of subjects or events. Longinotto's consistent use of *verité* filmmaking techniques in her work benefits from the historical trust associated with it. Her films allow her subjects the freedom to reveal themselves in their own way in as unmediated a fashion as possible.

Mediation is not completely absent in *cinéma verité*. It is evident that all films are edited to some degree, but this does not necessarily undermine ethics. As Pratap Rughani (2013: 107) notes: 'Audiences expect filmmakers to engage honestly with their subjects and to distil what they find.' This distillation involves choices, and audience trust is nurtured through the 'transparency that filmmakers show' (ibid). In essence, Rughani argues that trust is gained less from any rhetoric of neutrality – which can so often be a mirage – but by structural transparencies such as straightforward editing and an absence of the misleading distractions so often displayed in more structured realities. Longinotto's films certainly include transparencies of form through techniques such as hand-held filming and framing, the prioritisation of subjects' voices and the absence of any overt narrativisation techniques. While Longinotto does not physically appear in her own films, her presence is evidenced in editing choices that leave in moments of shaky focus, or snatches of informal conversations between herself and her subjects. The resulting style is one that prioritises an engagement between audiences and subjects rather than an authorial voice and, therefore, suggests itself as a perfect arena to bear witness to testimonies of experience and beliefs.

True crime in the 'post-truth' digital age

Conventions of the true crime documentary genre are not generally associated with any 'hallowed' filmmaking techniques. True crime is very often accused of sensationalism, over-dramatisation, misleading characterisation and the manipulation of emotional engagement through heavily narrativised content. In fact, Tanya Horeck argues: 'Many contemporary true crime texts are exercises in media manipulation' (2019: 10). She explains how the 'post-truth' digital age of Google searches and social media allows the packaging of true crime as 'entertainment products' (ibid: 11). The key term here is 'entertainment', a label that immediately disturbs notions of ethical responsibility and transparency in relation to the presentation of 'factual' information. While Horeck focuses on 'many' not 'all', it does reflect a general disdain towards the genre echoed in many academic studies. While I argue the genre is more diverse and serious than these accusations suggest, I do agree that the label 'true crime' is often associated with entertainment and that this labelling is likely to influence audience expectations and engagement. This is especially true when we account for the multiple competing narratives about true crime events that are easily found in a variety of media forms. For instance, the mafia wars in Sicily have generated countless narratives in books, films, television and countless online websites, communities and platforms. Any serious documentary that engages with topics of true crime competes with a variety of alternative formats that may well influence audiences' reactions to, or beliefs in the testimonies, or images presented.

The mafia wars

The history of the mafia in Sicily is complex, and much of its activity and character remains hidden or shrouded in myth. However, the period between the late 1970s and early 1990s unveiled more concrete information about mafia structures, motivations and actions than ever before. It is labelled 'the second' or 'the great' mafia war. A period of wide-ranging mafia violence in and around Palermo resulted in high-profile trials, the assassination of top Italian justices, including Giovanni Falcone and Paulo Borsellino, and unveiled evidence of state complicity in criminal activity. These events changed many people's perceptions of the mafia. For some, specifically those living in its shadow, it encouraged outrage and an organised and consistent resistance to its power. For others, especially those who consumed stories and images of the events from afar, it became a legendary period of mafia activity – frightening, yet fascinating in its levels of brutality and reach. Letizia Battaglia and her partner Franco Zecchin worked as photojournalists during this period and documented many of the key moments of violence. Battaglia's work is internationally recognised for its focus on victims' female relatives, or other onlookers, especially children. However, her initial motivation for such a focus was aimed primarily at a local audience, to encourage resistance to mafia activity. Alongside Zecchin, she organised spontaneous exhibitions of her photographs on the streets of Corleone, Sicily, in an attempt to break the tradition of silence that had long allowed mafia activity to continue unchallenged.

Paula Salvio (2017: 100) believes Battaglia's work is a testimony to anti-crime activism. She notes how Battaglia's self-described 'unintended archive' of mafia murders 'breaks silences and complicities with state and mafia corruption through storytelling and story-taking practices that operate apart from state control'. Her images counteract the state's narrative that suggested mafia violence as confined only to its immediate members by publicising the realities of widespread murder and intimidation. Since digitisation, Salvio argues, the archive continues to 'expand the arc of remembering' (ibid: 114), by giving the work a global reach. Battaglia passed away in 2022 just three years after the release of Longinotto's documentary. Therefore, the film stands as Battaglia's final testimony of her memories of her working life and the lasting legacy of her experiences witnessing and documenting mafia violence.

Testimony and victimhood
The title of Longinotto's film instantly suggests it as a true crime documentary. However, audiences that are more aware of her body of work may assume it to be an intimate character study, for that is her consistent filmic approach. Therefore, in order to examine the ethics of bearing witness I focus on two things: the evidence of true crime, such as archive footage and the focus on witnesses and victims rather than law enforcement; and the use of *verité* interview styles and how such informality affects subject testimony. I examine how the true crime topic interacts or infects the ways audiences are encouraged to engage with the central documentary subject and whether the *verité* style still empowers the voice in this context. Longinotto's style encourages her subjects to tell their stories in their own way, with minimal interference from the crew. In an interview about her earlier film *Rough aunties* (2008), Longinotto explains how she always has her camera ready but waits for her subjects to indicate they wish her to film (Thynne and Ali-Ali 2011). This contrasts with most techniques used in mainstream true crime for they tend to rely on more formal 'talking head' interviews and stylised re-enactments. Longinotto's focus on informal subject-led interviews emphasises the subject's autonomy at the point of filming. It also encourages a tone of intimate confession, or testimony, for the subject is allowed to speak in the manner and on topics they find most appropriate.

To explain the contrast between *verité* and more formal interview styles, I wish to draw attention to a BBC series, *Murder in the Badlands* (Birney and Byrne 2022), that also centres on the testimony of victims' families rather than on law enforcement, or the possible perpetrators of the crime. Focused on unsolved murders, the series gives most of the screentime to interviews with family members who describe their loved one, the events and the aftermath in intimate detail. This helps to keep the focus on the effects of crime more than the grisly details, forensic investigation or legal procedures. Allowing family members to speak at length in some ways helps to give a voice, bearing witness to the life and character of the victim.

At first glance it appears much more open and respectful of the personal tragedy that is often obscured in the usual media rush to explore the crime. However, in contrast to *verité* styles, the interviews in *Murder in the Badlands* are formal talking heads and the tone of the series, which features a poem read over the titles about women's fear of male violence, is one of sombre dread. The female victims are consistently described as 'at the mercy' of male predators, or – as the series focuses on the era of conflict in Northern Ireland – of political violence. The environments, titled 'Badlands' are conveyed as dangerous territory for women to live in or enter alone. In consequence, the subjects are empowered to talk about their experiences, but their testimony is framed within a general tone of victimhood and suffering. In short, the restrictions of television formatting that favours tones of intrigue and audience engagement dominates the style.

Longinotto's *verité* style avoids the above framing devices and allows the voice of her subject to dominate the narrative. In that sense, her film avoids the trappings of a true crime entertainment structure. However, her film does use a great deal of archive including still images of Battaglia's photographs, clips from fiction films, archive news footage of the mafia wars and subsequent trials. While the archive is necessary to provide historical context and evidence of her work, these inserts threaten the autonomy of the testimony. Embedding history within the testimony of witnesses, according to Martin Lucas (2017: 100), is a typical approach to significant historical events because 'there is a great deal of value placed on the authority imbued

George S. Larke-Walsh

by the accretion of individual experience in the form of "history from below"'.

However, because this tends to employ a compassionate approach to testimony and uses archive material merely to buttress rather than challenge it, Lucas argues such a subject is presented as a victim rather than an active witness. In other words, it does not invite audiences to question events or the subject's role within them. Plus, the focus on victimhood emphasises their otherness as it reduces them to the role of 'sufferer' rather than presenting them as a complex human being. Thus, the presence of archive in Longinotto's film may overwhelm Battaglia's spoken memories and reduce her testimony to simple victimhood. In essence, Lucas is arguing that too much guidance towards sympathy undermines the agency of the witness but, importantly, he does not view the subject's emotions as the problem.

Drawing from the work of anthropologist Joel Robbins (2013), Lucas argues it is the overly-sympathetic approach to victim testimony that undermines it and suggests, instead, that testimony of trauma should be left to speak for itself. He notes that empathising with a witness of trauma is a natural occurrence because 'we as observers and witnesses are secure in our abilities to know it when we see it and to feel empathy with those who suffer it' (ibid), while empathy also creates engagement through what Fassin and Rechtman (2009: 18), in their influential work on the shifts in attitudes towards survivors describe, as a 'communion in trauma'. Hence, accepting trauma as universally recognised allows other aspects of testimony to come to the fore, such as healing or activism. In short, a witness is allowed to be more than just a victim.

I agree that encouraging compassion does not restrict witness testimony to the role of victimhood. I have previously suggested that creating a sense of solidarity between the documentarian and subject, similar perhaps to a 'communion in trauma', can help to elevate the power of individual testimony, especially across cultures. I argue that 'the emotional qualities of Longinotto's work should be recognized as a key strength in their presentation of feminist solidarity' (op cit: 149). However, it is fair to ask if a focus on compassion works in all cases; is it part of the film-making practice or does it require specific combinations of testimony, evidence and editing for it to succeed? In other words, should we really be arguing about the merits of particular stylistic choices, or is that just a distraction from the reality that bearing witness to testimonies of trauma and memories of significant historical events is such an individualised experience that any testimony – and indeed any audience response to the topic – is contradictory?

This paper cannot solve such debates: what I offer is an explanation for why true crime is virtually impossible to present in a consistent manner, especially in terms of emotion and this is, perhaps, why the genre is mistrusted. Furthermore, it can only ever be presented in historical terms, i.e. the events that cause it to be labelled as crime have passed and the media text is constructed from evidence of those affected. Hence, a focus on emotions that include victimhood and suffering is unavoidable and should be recognised as such rather than viewed as a hindrance, or a fault in the storytelling approach. Rather, it is important to focus on how emotion is conveyed through the combination of voices derived from testimony, archive and so on, and whether those affected by crime are allowed the freedom to express their responses to events in a fully-rounded manner on screen.

Shooting the mafia
Mafia documentaries are, by nature of the topic, about 'organised crime' and provide studies of environments and networks of events. To this end, Longinotto's film is as much about true crime as it is about Battaglia, as the surrounding criminal environment and events impact on every aspect of the narrative. In essence, the film is a character study of Letizia Battaglia providing information on her life, loves, career and activism. However, all of her life is influenced by the presence of the mafia in her hometown of Palermo, Sicily. Extreme patriarchal attitudes and fear of crime kept her housebound from a young age; then her husband refused to allow her to have a life beyond bearing children. Her love affairs broke the marriage and led to her work on the local newspaper, *L'Ora*, her photojournalism, her political career and continued grassroots activism. Her entire life is affected by the mafia and the consequences of this remain unresolved.

While the film appears constructed from two extensive informal interviews, it also includes a great deal of archive footage, some of which is intrinsic in adding visual evidence to her memories of events, but some is authorial adding emotional cues to characterisation. The film is only *cinéma verité* in terms of its interviews and a few sections of observational footage. Hence, the ethics of bearing witness lies not only in how those interviews are framed but how they are placed within the context of the surrounding archive. Within the interviews it is evident that Battaglia is responding to questions or prompts unheard in the film as she occasionally asks: 'Why are you making me think about this?', or 'I could talk about it, but I don't want to.' Another structuring device in the interviews involves Battaglia chatting to old friends, such as her ex-lovers Santi and Franco, as well as her personal assistant, Maria Chiara Di Trapani. These encounters still feel like testimony but are revealed through the informalities of conversation and shared memory. This style also emphasises the emotional aspects of her testimony and shared memories in that Battaglia often asks her friends how they feel, such as when she asks Franco why he finds revisiting Palermo so 'heart breaking'.

A final structural point to note is that formal interviews with people connected to Battaglia are interspersed throughout the film. These and other observational footage provide information on her continued reputation as an outspoken anti-mafia activist as well as opinions on her actions and personality. They are an important aspect to the consideration of ethics of testimony, for their inclusion provides an opportunity to hear competing opinions about her life and her work, thus creating a more rounded characterisation.

For the first thirty minutes of the film the mafia remains in the shadows. Battaglia talks of her early life, her father's over-protective behaviour and her first marriage. She describes how her life was blighted by 'that awful man in the shadows'. By this she means the prevalence of machismo and poverty in Sicily that influenced so many of the aggressive behaviours blighting women's lives. The film intercuts Battaglia's interview with archive documentary footage describing widespread poverty and cultural attitudes, but also images from fiction film that suggest Italian femininity as sexually permissive. The song 'Volare' ('Fly') accompanies images from Battaglia's marriage and emphasises her explanation of why she had affairs. It is evident that by the time she began her career as a photojournalist, Battaglia had a reputation for wayward behaviour. The film constructs this almost as a romantic myth that glosses over the violence and trauma that must have occurred. It also avoids discussing her children. She says: 'I could talk a lot about, but I don't want to.' By the time we get to the 'dark, painful time' (namely the almost twenty years of 'the great mafia war'), the film has built a portrait of Battaglia that echoes the culture surrounding her. In essence, Battaglia seems as brazen, courageous and damaged as Sicily itself.

The construction of character helps to create a balance between Battaglia the activist and the mafia violence that dominates the rest of the film. While, this characterisation is achieved through conscious editing and the manipulation of facts, it is evident this is the character she wishes to present to the world. Battaglia's testimony suggests herself as a victim of the mafia when she says: 'You can never be truly happy when you've lived through that horror.' However, she is also angry, calling the mafia boss, Totò Riina who organised the assassination of Judge Giovanni Falcone, in May 1992, a 'shabby moron'. Battaglia's testimony is a complex mix of lamentation and defiance. She mourns for the victims and the violence she has witnessed, but she refuses to see any glamour in the 'cruel power' the mafia bosses have displayed over the years.

Allowing contradictions

In the early part of the film, Battaglia states her desire to burn the negatives of her most famous images. The reasons for this are implied in her words 'I want to take away the beauty that others see in them. I want to destroy them'. However, later in the film she states: 'The photos I never took hurt me the most. I never took them. I miss them.' None of her interview statements are altered, examined or challenged by voice-over or added imagery. Her thoughts are allowed to remain as they appear. They are ambiguous or contradictory not because of any intention to obscure the truth, but because her testimony, like all memories, is an ever-evolving process. When discussing Falcone's death, she asks: 'Why are you making me think about this? I don't want to. I realise now, I've never been at peace. It's always been like this. My life has always been a struggle.' The process of remembering and explaining events is witnessed here as an emotional activity and we are guided to recognise Battaglia's memories as complex and difficult to describe in simple or stable terms.

Longinotto's films are described as ethnographic in nature because of her consistent focus on individuals who invite us to connect with their lives as lived. The global success of her films, no matter if her subjects are British, American, Iranian, Japanese or Indian, lies in the fact that she acknowledges their cultural individualities while still managing to capture points of universal connection. To do this, her camera bears witness to their unique stories rather than imposing a pre-defined characterisation. Joel Robbins (2013: 455), writing for the Royal Anthropological Institute, suggests there is:

> ... a way of writing ethnography in which we do not primarily provide cultural context so as to offer lessons in how lives are lived differently elsewhere, but in which we offer accounts of trauma that make us and our readers feel in our bones the vulnerability we as human beings all share.

Longinotto practises informal visual ethnography, but the unique topic of *Shooting the mafia* challenges that because it demands more than the usual amount of archive footage to intrude upon Battaglia's testimony. The images and news footage used operate as true crime elements whose universal voice threatens to overwhelm the uniqueness of her individual experience and infect it with the entertainment value of true crime intrigue. Battaglia also struggles to control the tone of the narrative because the topic remains unresolved in her mind. Her contradictory testimony that alternates between pain and defiance means audiences are inevitably drawn to empathise with the emotional impact these events have had on her life. The over-arching tone is lamentation at the human cost of the mafia wars and the continued acquiescence of the Italian political system to the mafia's influence. In her concluding remarks Battaglia states: 'I dream of seeing a Sicily free of the mafia', thus acknowledging the fact that the battle continues.

The focus on Battaglia's defiant and individualised testimony to the events of the great mafia war does challenge conventions of true crime in *Shooting the mafia*, but it does not entirely erase their presence, nor their power to influence audience responses. It is understandable that Battaglia would want to destroy some of her photographs for the beauty people see in them, as their visual power in the film is such a loud challenge to the tone of the film. They are innately sensational. Similarly, Battaglia's own testimony of the 'cruel power' she witnessed in mafia behaviour and her own suffering after so many deaths suggest her character as imbued with victimhood and suffering. We are also invited to empathise with the levels of trauma faced by women who lost husbands and sons as well as the national trauma of the violent deaths of judges Falcone and Borsellino. Longinotto cannot avoid sensationalising the topic when the sensational enormity of events speaks so loudly in all the archive and trauma that surrounds it.

Conclusions

Battaglia's contradictory testimony, oscillating between despair and defiance, and between the desire to show and the desire to forget, is a testament to Longinotto's ethical filmmaking practices. She allows the contradictions to remain in the testimony and refuses to persuade audiences to feel a particular way. She does not add voice-over or sombre music, as used in regular true crime, to signal audience sympathies or exaggerate a sense of trauma. However, this does not mean she can avoid a focus on the suffering subject, because that suffering is evident in Battaglia's own words. In bearing witness to her testimony, the film provides insight into the realities of life lived in a society blighted by mafia activity. The realities of who and what defines the mafia remain steadfastly unresolved as a battleground of competing voices. This is evidenced in the archival material of images of the dead, interviews with mafia bosses and victims of their violence, news footage and clips from fictional films. However, Longinotto's choice to have Battaglia as the central subject prioritises her viewpoint. Furthermore, the intercutting of interview and archive suggests Battaglia as a personification of the broader societal experience which can be characterised as an oscillation between victimhood and defiance.

The influence of the 'men in the shadows' that Battaglia describes early in the film stays true to the end. Battaglia may call them buffoons or morons, but their status as the epitome of organised criminal power has a global reach. The ethics of ethnography (see Robbins 2013) suggests the listening to testimony needs to include a 'motive for change' in order to provide agency to the voice. Longinotto's film certainly includes that in its focus on the street protests and social defiance against the police and politicians who are accused of doing nothing to protect anti-mafia judges. It allows us to view Battaglia as a fully-rounded, complex human being, rather than a symbol of victimhood, refusing to soften her image as committed to career and activism above family. Her chain-smoking, openly rebellious character refuses to offer anything but plain truths as she sees them, regardless of the innate contradictions that are included in such a subjective testimony.

Hence, I argue subject testimony can challenge the entertainment value of true crime if, instead of framing it as entirely victimhood, it accepts trauma as universally understood and thus allows other aspects – beyond suffering – to emerge. Longinotto's *verité* style is an effective choice in this case in that its informal style undercuts the true crime conventions that tend to prioritise goal-oriented narratives and clearly defined emotional cues. This does not mean the film avoids sensationalising mafia activity. The mystique of the mafia remains strong enough to withstand individual testimony and so the intrigue that surrounds the seemingly irresolvable nature of mafia activity is not fully undermined by this one documentary. However, *Shooting the mafia* effectively champions the activism of Battaglia, alongside judges, other journalists, victims and the general population of Sicily. This documentary is a valid attempt to undermine the glamorisation of the mafia that dominates most media and so often drowns out the voice of victims. It bears witness to the tireless work of many to unveil its cruelties and offer a loud challenge to its codes of silence.

References

Birney, Trevor and Byrne, Brendan (2022) *Murder in the Badlands* Fine Point Films, UK

Fassin, Didier and Rechtman, Richard (2009) *The empire of trauma: An inquiry into the condition of victimhood*, Princeton, Princeton University Press

Horeck, Tanya (2019) *Justice on demand: True crime in the digital streaming era*, Detroit, Wayne State University Press

Larke-Walsh, George S. (2019) Compassion in Kim Longinotto's documentary practice, *Feminist Media Studies,* Vol.19, No. 1 pp 147-160

Lucas, Martin (2017) Documentary: Trauma and an ethics of knowing, *Post Script*, Vol. 36, Nos. 2-3 pp 98-116

Nichols, Bill (2016) *Speaking truths with film: Evidence, ethics, politics in documentary*, Oakland, University of California Press

Robbins, Joel (2013) Beyond the suffering subject: Toward an anthropology of the good, *Journal of the Royal Anthropological Institute*, Vol. 19, No. 3 pp 447-462

Rughani, Pratap (2013) The dance of documentary ethics, Winston, Brian (ed.) *The documentary film book*, London, Palgrave Macmillan pp 89-109

Salvio, Paula M. (2017) *The story-takers: Public pedagogy, transitional justice and Italy's non-violent protest against the mafia*, Toronto, University of Toronto Press

Spence, Louise and Navarro, Vinicius (2011) *Crafting truth: Documentary form and meaning*, New Brunswick, Rutgers University Press

Thynne, Lizzie and Ali-Ali, Nadje (2011) An interview with Kim Longinotto, *Feminist Review*, Vol. 99 pp 26-28

Williams, Linda (2016) Mirrors without memories: Truth, history, and the new documentary, Kahana, Jonathan (ed.) *The documentary film reader: History, theory, criticism*, Oxford, Oxford University Press

Winston, Brian (2005) Ethics, Rosenthal, Alan and Corner, John (eds) *New challenges for documentary*, New York, Manchester University Press, second edition pp 181-193

Note on the contributor

George S. Larke-Walsh (PhD) is a faculty member in Arts and Creative Industries at the University of Sunderland. She began her academic career in the northeast area of the UK, but then moved to the USA, teaching at the University of North Texas from 2004 to 2020. Her scholarly interests focus on non-fiction and fiction film theories. Her publishing history includes books and articles on ethics in true crime, as well as the presentation of mythologies and masculine identities in narratives about the mafia.

Conflict of interest

There was no conflict of interest in the production of this research.

PAPER

Ilse A. Ras

Sympathetic or blame-worthy: The handling of ethical complexities in reporting on the victims of the 'Essex lorry deaths' by Dutch online-only news sources

Trafficked migrants are, legally, victims. Smuggled migrants are, generally speaking, not. In practice, however, identifying whether a person is one or the other proves complex, especially at the border. Misidentification has serious consequences, as it can lead to the criminalisation of those who would more properly be regarded as victims. Such difficulties present themselves to investigators, e.g., the police, but also to reporting media. How do the media negotiate these legal and ethical complexities in their reporting? Through a combined content and critical stylistic analysis, understood within a framework of critical discourse analysis, this paper inductively identifies the types of representation of victims in Dutch online-only news sources' reporting on the 'Essex lorry deaths', when 39 people were found dead in the back of a refrigerated lorry. Was this a case of people smuggling (gone wrong) or of human trafficking? By representing the deceased as passive objects, as though they were (unexpected) cargo, Dutch online-only news sources, rather than negotiate this question, largely sidestep it and the various ethical complexities associated with it. This, in turn, allows these media outlets to avoid discussing broader systemic issues that render these people especially vulnerable to exploitation, regardless of the classification of the acts associated with their movement, that in this case led to their deaths, as either 'smuggling' or 'trafficking'.

Keywords: human trafficking, people smuggling, content analysis, critical discourse analysis, online-only news

Introduction
In 2019 two teenage Vietnamese boys escaped to Belgium from a Dutch asylum-seeker facility. Dutch and Belgian prosecutors decided not to recapture these boys, but track where they received help, so Dutch and Belgian police could try to trace and dismantle a European people-smuggling network. However, they lost track of the boys. Eventually, on 23 October, they turned up – in the back of a refrigerated lorry in Grays, Essex, United Kingdom, along with 37 other Vietnamese nationals. All had died during the journey across the Channel and into England.

This event, now known as the 'Essex lorry deaths', received media coverage in the UK and across Europe (Gregoriou, Ras and Muzdeka 2021). It was necessary for the police investigation to determine demographic characteristics, such as gender/sex, age, ethnicity and, where possible, name, to be able to track those who were responsible for this tragedy. The prosecution also needed to ascertain the specific role of the victims, to determine the actual crime. This is a complex legal question, because the two main options in this case – human trafficking or facilitating people smuggling – are very different concepts in relation to the question of victim participation and responsibility. Human trafficking inherently means exploitation, whereas in smuggling, exploitation is an aggravating factor – and victimisation only occurs as a result of that exploitation, not of the smuggling. It is also a complex ethical question because it touches on the politically sensitive issue of migration, as well as concerns around global economic inequality and access to opportunities.

It is generally assumed that media framing of any topic influences public views and responses. The presented narrative of the topic indirectly or directly, legitimises or directs policy on that topic (Sobel 2014; Van Liempt 2011). Furthermore, this presentation may also directly influence action: Gonzalez-Pons et al. (2020), for instance, show that sex trafficking myths, e.g., those that fit with the dominant narrative, often pushed by various media, hamper professionals' ability to accurately identify genuine trafficking victims. It is, therefore, important to examine media representations of cases of migration and human trafficking. Such representations consist not only of the topic selection, i.e., the 'what' of the story, often determined by the newsworthiness of the event (see Galtung and Ruge 1965), but also of the topic framing (Goffman 1974), i.e., the 'how' of the representation, such as word choice. The current study aims to develop a typology of victim representations to facilitate a future identification of frames in this reporting.

In recently examined European reporting on the 'Essex lorry deaths' in traditional print media (Gregoriou et al. 2021), there appear to be two approaches to the victims of this crime. In one, these victims are held responsible for their own deaths; in the other it is suggested that these people were perhaps attempting to escape desperate circumstances, in search of a better life. This distinction appears closely linked to discussions focusing on whether they were likely to have been the victims of traffickers, or of people smuggling gone wrong (ibid). The current paper examines reporting in online-only media, defined by the lack of offline outputs (such as newspapers or television channels) and much-used below-the-line comments sections, to facilitate comparisons between news genres in their reporting of this specific event. This paper focuses on how these online-only outlets portray these victims throughout the course of the case and negotiate the legal and ethical difficulties relating to the question of the victims' role(s) in this case.

Narratives of trafficking versus smuggling

The *Protocol to prevent, suppress and punish trafficking in persons especially women and children, supplementing the United Nations Convention against Transnational Organised Crime*,[1] more commonly known as the *Palermo protocol*, adopted by the UN in 2000, identifies 'human trafficking' as the movement of persons without their consent (or using methods that invalidate any consent these persons may have given) 'for the purpose of exploitation'. Children, i.e., under-18, cannot in any case, consent to any movement relating to exploitation. Given the location of discovery of the victims in the 'Essex lorry deaths' case, the relevant national legislation is the UK Modern Slavery Act (2015) which similarly defines trafficking as arranging or facilitating 'the travel of another person ('V') with a view to V being exploited', sidestepping potential questions of consent by indicating that it is 'irrelevant whether V consents to the travel (whether V is an adult or a child)'. Both define 'exploitation' as forced (sexual) labour for commercial purposes, whereby it is made clear that *any* sexual labour carried out by children (for commercial purposes) is exploitation. Other forms of labour may be permitted (and thus are not considered exploitation), as long as consent (as in these matters defined by national legislation) is present and labour conditions are in line with national legislation relating to labour performed by children. Whilst 'travel' is understood in a very broad sense, human trafficking tends to be understood as a transnational offence, i.e., involving border crossing by, at least, the trafficked.

People smuggling is defined through a different *Palermo protocol*, commonly known as the *Smuggling protocol*: the *Protocol against the smuggling of migrants by land, sea and air, supplementing the United Nations Convention against Transnational Organised Crime.*[2] It states people smuggling as benefiting from the facilitation of crossing the border into a state without the migrant 'complying with the necessary requirements for legal entry', for instance through fraud (e.g. fake passports) or through concealed border crossing (e.g. in a lorry). Exploitation 'along the way' does not make it a trafficking offence but is a potentially aggravating circumstance. Human trafficking inherently entails the exploitation and, therefore, victimisation, of people; people smuggling does not. However, the journey is clearly as dangerous as the destination, for both groups. Indeed, smuggled migrants may just as much become the victim of crimes such as physical and sexual abuse, fraud or, as in the Essex lorry deaths, manslaughter/murder. This legally renders them victims, albeit not of human trafficking. However, as Van Liempt (2011) argues, the distinction between trafficking and smuggling is both problematic and unhelpful, not only due to the above complexities, but also as it ignores the very pressing reasons individuals might have for attempting to migrate and becoming vulnerable to exploitation (either at the destination or along the journey), and fails to acknowledge the complexity of many of these journeys.

Problematically, many of those identified as migrants also end up criminalised. While the *Smuggling protocol* indicates that migrants 'shall not become liable to criminal prosecution', national legislation often nonetheless criminalises them, because they are often held to be in violation of immigration laws. In the UK, this encompasses all people who have not received leave to enter or stay in the UK according to the Immigration Act (1971) or any other

Ilse A. Ras

of the UK's immigration rules. Migrants trafficked to the UK are, technically, similarly in violation of the immigration rules but, following the Modern Slavery Act (2015), those identified as victims of trafficking are not prosecuted for breach of these rules. In short, those identified as smuggled are criminalised; those identified as trafficked are not. The tendency to portray migrants negatively, or even criminally, either through an over-sampling of stories featuring criminalised migrants, or through a representation of migrants as criminal, is also observed in the media, for instance in Dutch (Brouwer et al. 2017) and British newspapers (Gabrielatos and Baker 2008; KhosraviNik 2010).

In media reporting, then, we might expect sympathy for trafficking victims (non-consensually moved), whereas smuggled migrants (consensually moved) are presumably more likely to be victim-blamed. Migrants' ability to give informed consent is a key distinguishing feature between the two crimes, but difficult to prove. Often other, technically irrelevant case and victim characteristics are drawn on instead to determine the initial crime, i.e., to answer the question of consent. Two characteristics relating to exploitation are gender and the type of labour for which a person is exploited. Lobasz (2009: 339) argues that males in particular are more substantially misidentified as smuggled, especially those exploited for non-sexual labour, rather than trafficked. Van Liempt (2011) explores further complexities in the pattern of gendered assumptions that seem to underlie official policy decisions regarding the identification of migrating persons. Arguably, such tendencies could be the result of the dominant narrative of what human trafficking *really* or *ideally* is, and what irregular migration is, with the consequences of again reinforcing those dominant narratives.

The narrative of trafficking contains a very specific interpretation of who is (and is not) a *real/ideal* victim of human trafficking. This is a story in which young (Eastern European or Asian) girls are violently transported across borders and, at their (Western) destination, sexually exploited (Sanford et al. 2016; Farrell and Fahy 2009; Gregoriou and Ras 2018). In short, these are *ideal* victims (see Christie 1986). While this group does form a substantial share of the reported-on victims, many other genuine victims – for example, those trafficked for labour exploitation – are less likely recognised as victims because of the dominance of this representation of human trafficking. In consequence, they do not receive the support that is made available to those who *are* recognised as victims (Gregoriou and Ras 2018). In fact, they are likely identified as irregular migrants, smuggled, and thus end up criminalised, as described above. As such, while victims fitting the mould of the ideal victim are more likely presented as undeserving of victimisation, deserving of – indeed *requiring* – government support, there are different representations of victims/migrants in human trafficking and people smuggling reporting, especially when these victims/migrants do not and cannot be made to fit into the mould of the ideal victim. Given these complexities, there are various strategies employed by news outlets to describe victims, depending on their interpretation of the case. This study aims to inductively identify and categorise these representations.

Methods
Data collection
News items were collected between 1 June 2021 and 25 March 2022, from Dutch online-only news sources (Bakker 2018), two of which, *Nu.nl* and *GeenStijl.nl*, published items relating to this event (the others, which have a more niche focus, have not). The search terms used were generated through snowballing, with the resultant list of (translated) search terms: *Grays, Essex, lorry drama, lorry, refrigerated lorry, 39 dead, Essex lorry deaths, lorry driver, human trafficking, people smuggling, human traffickers, people smugglers, sea container.*

Hits on these websites were manually assessed for relevance in a two-stage process, whereby first titles were screened, with full-text screening of remaining articles. Relevant articles were those in which reference was made to multiple identifying characteristics of this case, such as the number of victims, the job and nationality of the primary suspect/offender, and the location of discovery. Some 24 relevant articles were identified.

The collected items are specified in Table 1. Roughly 60 per cent of these articles were published in the first month following this case; a third were published in the first week.

Table 1: Overview of included articles

ID	Date	Time	Com.	Source[1]	Title [Translated by the author]
1	23-10-2019	10:49	2	NU	39 bodies found in lorry in United Kingdom
23	23-10-2019	10:50	209	GS	English police find 39 corpses in sea container
2	24-10-2019	01:15	5	NU	Identification of 39 bodies in lorry started, Northern Irish houses searched
3	24-10-2019	12:07	32	NU	39 deceased persons in lorry in England were Chinese
4	25-10-2019	13:38	1	NU	Two new arrests in investigation into deaths in lorry UK
5	26-10-2019	16:29	39	NU	Driver lorry with 39 dead prosecuted for manslaughter
6	27-10-2019	13:39	11	NU	Three suspects in case 39 dead in lorry UK free on bail
7	28-10-2019	19:58	2	NU	'Global people smuggling gang behind 39 dead in lorry'
15	1-11-2019	15:16	0	NU	Second Northern Irish man arrest for manslaughter 39 people in lorry
16	4-11-2019	04:51	1	NU	British police assume 39 dead in trailer are Vietnamese
17	4-11-2019	08:39	14	NU	Six further arrests in Vietnam in case of 39 dead in British trailers
18	7-11-2019	15:22	2	NU	British police: All deceased in lorry were Vietnamese
8	22-11-2019	12:09	10	NU	Another man from Northern Ireland arrested for 39 dead in lorry
19	23-11-2019	06:17	55	NU	Dead person in British lorry disappeared from Dutch asylum facility
20	11-2-2020	15:22	7	NU	Suspects arrested for death 39 Vietnamese in lorry England
21	8-4-2020	17:14	0	NU	British driver admits guilt in deaths 39 Vietnamese in lorry
22	21-4-2020	00:06	0	NU	New arrest in British case of 39 dead Vietnamese in lorry
9	27-5-2020	17:13	4	NU	People smuggling gang arrested in Belgium and France for lorry drama UK
10	30-5-2020	12:05	35	NU	Suspected head of people smuggling gang relating to lorry drama UK arrested
14	16-7-2020	09:22	157	NU	'Dutch prosecutors asked Belgium not to intervene in case of runaway teenagers lorry drama UK'
13	18-7-2020	10:44	144	NU	Belgium: Dutch prosecutors did not ask to leave victims lorry drama alone after all
12	15-9-2020	09:41	12	NU	Suspects in case of lorry drama UK convicted to 7.5 years in jail
11	21-12-2020	15:45	0	NU	Two men found guilty of manslaughter in case of lorry drama UK

Analysis

The inductive content analysis (Hsieh and Shannon 2005) of these 24 news articles began using Atlas.ti 9, aimed at systematically determining the key persons/types of persons, locations and actions covered. This coding was carried out on a sentential level. Subsequently, the representation topics of particular interest, e.g., those types of persons recurring with great frequency across all articles, in this specific case primary and secondary victims, were stylistically analysed following the approach set out by Jeffries (2010). Particular attention was paid to:

1. Naming and describing (Jeffries 2010: 17-36) of victims, such as the labels (including metaphorical (Lakoff and Johnson 1980) and metonymical) used to indicate these people, as well as pre- and post-modifying phrases.

2. The grammatical agency, also known as transitivity (Jeffries 2010: 37-50), of these people; are they actors or acted upon?

3. Relatedly, the types of actions in which these people are involved (ibid); if they are actors, what do they do, and are these intentional actions?

4. Specific subsections of process types are those relating to communication and thought, analysed through speech, writing and thought presentation (ibid: 130-145, see also Short 2012), whereby key questions include 'whose words are reproduced in this text, and how faithfully' and 'who is talked, written and thought *about*?'

Answering these questions allows us to systematically assess the representation of these victims. Developments in these representation types can also be tracked over time.

Findings

Key persons

Victims are the most often mentioned actors in these articles, trailed at some distance by suspects/offenders and law enforcement actors. Of the 252 references to victims, 227 are to primary victims, and 25 are to secondary victims, primarily family members. Figure 1 shows that while the attention given to primary victims throughout time fluctuates, it never does so especially drastically. However, we do see that after the first month primary victim mentions fluctuate between zero and five; mentions of secondary victims drop to zero.

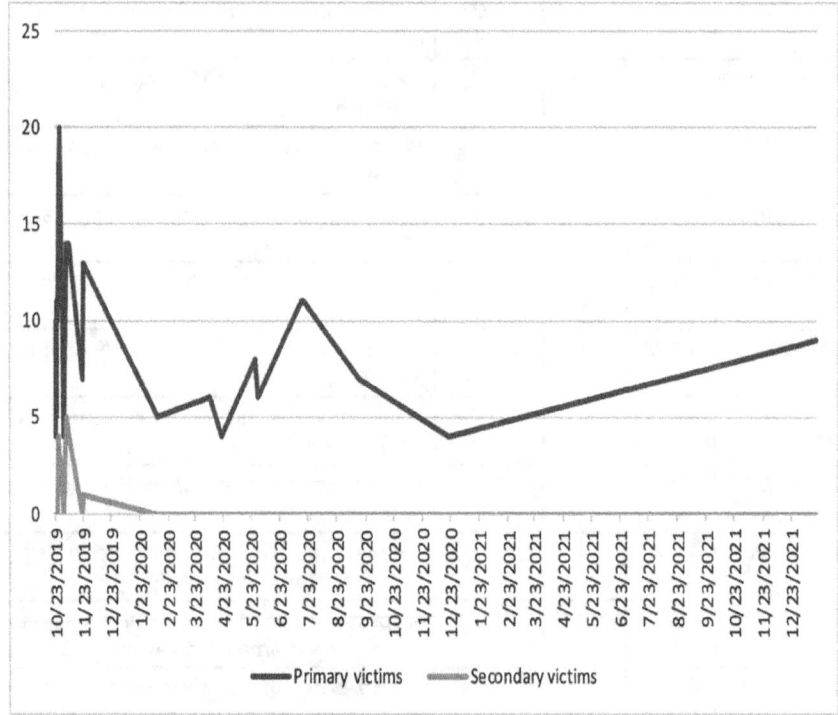

Figure 1: References to victims over time

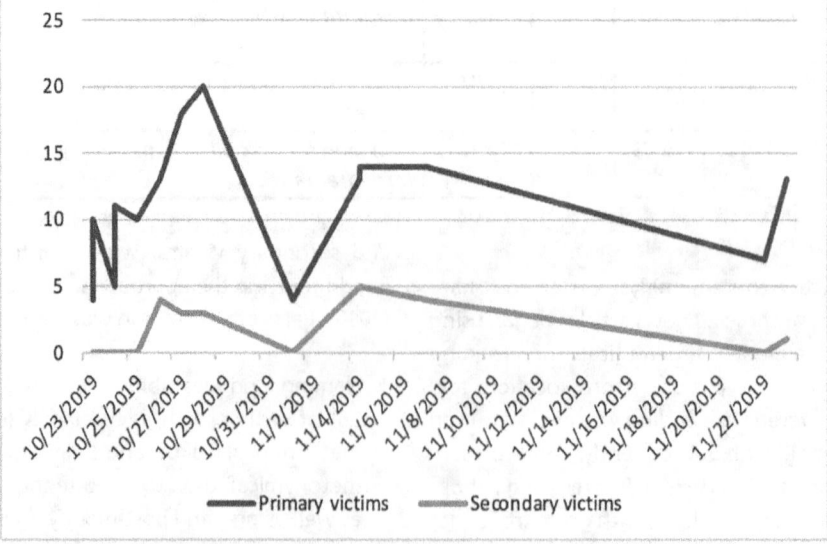

Figure 2: References to victims in the first month

What Figure 2 clearly shows, however, is a peak in discussions on the primary victims on 27 and 28 October 2019. These are extensive articles, describing, among other matters, the efforts taken by the Vietnamese government to identify these victims through DNA samples.

Victim descriptions
Primary victims
In the description of primary victims, we see the following details mentioned:

- group size;
- age;
- nationality;
- gender/sex;
- criminal justice role (as 'victim').

Furthermore, these victims are often described as 'bodies' or 'corpses', rather than as human beings, suggesting an element of objectification. This objectification is further underpinned through the description of these people as the subject in passive sentences and object in active sentences (the 'goal', in Hallidayan transitivity terms); and described processes as material, intentional actions, often carried out by police, more rarely by the suspects/offenders. They are also often verbiage in spoken processes and the phenomenon in mental processes, meaning that they are talked and thought about. When they do have agency, it is in supervention processes. Processes in which the described action is not a material, intentional action but instead something that 'just happens', such as 'dying', or in relational processes, in which these victims are described as carrying certain attributes (e.g., 'were female'). In other words, victims do not *do* – they are *done to*. This suggests a primary victim representation in which these victims are linguistically reduced to smuggled/trafficked cargo.

Secondary victims
Secondary victims are described as part of the Vietnamese community, or in familial relation to the primary victims ('several parents', 'the mother of the 18-year-old Hoang van Tiep'). They, too, tend to be the goal of material intentional actions, and part of some other person's verbiage, but, in contrast to primary victims, are rarely actors in non-intentional processes. Furthermore, occasionally, secondary victims' words are reported; when they are, this is done indirectly. Whilst this may be the result of translation, in contrast, (English) police officers' words are, at times, presented in direct speech, despite translation, for the Dutch audiences of these outlets.

In short, these linguistic trends suggest two main representation types for secondary victims, relating to the level of agency these relatives exercise. The following section further substantiates these identified representation types and adds new representation types where the currently identified representation types do not fit.

Victim representations
Primary victims
Unexpected cargo in lorry trailer (passive victims)
As is also clear from earlier descriptions, primary victims in Dutch online-only reports on this case are largely passive, even objectified as 'bodies' or 'dead' rather than 'people'. This objectifying representation of victims is by far the most dominant, and describes these victims as objects; bodies, found in a place they should not be in. Grammatically, this is a type of representation in which victims have no agency; mere goals of material actions by either police (in trying to identify these people) or unknown agents (in finding these victims; these are agentless passives). As these are mostly passive sentences, the focus is on these victims and the actions carried out in relation to them, rather than on the agents carrying out these actions. In relation to the police action of trying to identify them, these victims are subjects in relational processes, meaning that their characteristics are described, for example '39 dead persons in lorry in England *were* Chinese'. The erroneous yet confident categorical nature of this assertion also raises questions about the assumptions made by the police and media in identifying these and similar victims. This description is explicitly attributed to the police, making these active sentences the verbalisation (or implicitly verbalised, explicitly described as a phenomenon in a mental process, e.g., 'police suspect') of police processes. In short, these people are described here in a dehumanising manner, similar to how cargo might be described. Noteworthily absent in this representation is the question of how these victims ended up where they were found, and even how they died. As such, questions around responsibility/consent and crime are sidestepped. This representation is especially dominant in the first month of reporting, although it recurs across the whole corpus.

Victim of circumstances (active victims – supervention)
A second representation is one in which the humanity of these victims *is* acknowledged, through labels such as 'people' and 'victims', and through further descriptors of demographic factors, such as age, gender and nationality.

This is where these victims are described as dying (and, often, what the cause of death is). A key difference with the previous representation is that in the previous representation, these victims are labelled as dead ('the dead'); in the current representation, 'having died' is a modifier. This difference gives more room for questions around cause of death. Indeed, in many of these sentences we see attention for circumstances leading to these people's deaths, such as 'they had been in the refrigerated trailer of the lorry for ten hours before being discovered' and 'the Vietnamese probably died of a combination of a lack of oxygen and overheating in a closed-off space'. Furthermore, the use of the 'victim' label suggests that someone, other than these victims, must be held accountable for their deaths.

Occasionally, but rarely, are the actors held responsible for these deaths also explicitly mentioned in these sentences, as 'gangs', and 'a group of people smugglers'. In the case of the two runaways boys, the articles suggest perhaps the Dutch Prosecutors Office shares some responsibility. It is initially suggested by the Belgian Minister for Justice, and later denied by multiple actors, that Dutch prosecutors requested that Belgian police not intervene and return these boys to the Netherlands. While this representation acknowledges that a crime occurred, through the focus on the responsibility for the deaths of these people, again the question of whether this is human trafficking or migration gone wrong is largely sidestepped. This representation is largely absent from the first month of reporting. But then, the overall dominance of a dehumanising representation of these people as akin to 'unexpected cargo', suggests that this representation is only deployed after more information about the case, including the identities of these victims and more precise circumstances of their deaths, is shared.

Willing migrant (active victims – intentional)
One exception to the notion that these people are passive objects are the words of Mayor De Fauw of Zeebrugge, who indicates that these were active migrants. He says: 'It is improbable that the group entered the trailer just before departure.' The context in which the comment is made suggests that De Fauw believes that the people entered the trailer before it reached Zeebrugge. It is also mentioned but not attributed to any specific person, that 'the victims would have paid thousands of euros to people smugglers to enter Great Britain'. Similar suggestions, that these were willing migrants, are also made more implicitly in these articles, by equating them to the offenders' other clients, as in: 'Europol suspects that the migrant smugglers have transported dozens of people every day for the last few months'. Note here also the use of a collective noun, 'group' by De Fauw to refer to these people, and to the phrase 'dozens of people', reported as a Europol suspicion. Furthermore, the association of this case with other cases of irregular migration (gone wrong) – such as the explicit reference to the 'Perry Wacker case', better known as the 'Dover lorry deaths', from 2000, in which 58 Chinese migrants were found dead in a lorry (driven by Dutchman Perry Wacker) in Dover – implies that this is a recurring issue. Such descriptors tap into prevalent migration discourses whereby migrants are (metaphorically) described as a large, threatening mass (e.g., Gabrielatos and Baker 2008; Brouwer et al. 2017).

In other words, there is at least an undercurrent of ascription of consent (and, therefore, responsibility for their own deaths) to these victims. As this representation is explicitly attributed to external parties, it is argued that the reporting media outlet distances itself from this representation, although this would raise questions as to why these quotes are included in the first place. The ambiguity presented by this representation, in short, creates plausible deniability – in either direction. The two runaway boys are also actors in material intentional actions, specifically 'running away'. Noteworthily, these active sentences are not attributed to external parties, suggesting a more direct attribution of responsibility to these boys for their misfortune. This representation is clustered in a small number of articles.

Secondary victims
Secondary victims are only described in a small number of articles in general, in the first week after discovery and again when identification efforts begin to include DNA research, in the second week after discovery. Secondary victims are afterwards not referred to again.

The worried parent (active relatives)
These are secondary victims defined by their parental role ('several parents') to the victims ('their children'), as well as pro-action in communicating their belief that something may have happened to their children. This representation is present whenever secondary victims are referred to.

The police contact (passive relatives)
As the links between secondary and primary victims are, officially, unclear, descriptors for this group remain similarly cautious: not only are they labelled 'relatives' or 'the Vietnamese community', rather than more specific indicators (as with worried parents), these descriptors are further modified through epistemic ele-

ments ('potential', 'probable', 'presumable'). A key identifying element is their relation to other actors in these articles; specifically, they are consistently the goal or receiver of police material intentional or verbal processes: 'On Sunday, the Vietnamese police took DNA samples of the potential relatives of victims'; 'Police did indicate they would stay in close contact with the Vietnamese community.' After the victims are identified, relatives (no longer epistemically modified) again are the receivers of police verbal processes: 'The relatives of the victims have been informed.' This representation only begins after it is reported that the police are including DNA research in their identification efforts and is, therefore, context dependent.

Premature relatives (grammatically absent relatives)

What is noteworthy is the matter-of-factness with which the other secondary victims are reported. It seems taken for granted that parents missing their children would sound the alarm and stay in touch with the police whilst investigations are under way. However, as the current representation suggests, secondary victims should wait until they are given all the facts before they start expressing and acting on emotions other than worry, including holding memorial services. The unexpectedness of the timing of these actions is expressed through words such as 'already', as well as change-of-state processes combined with a contrasting conjunction, 'however, the identification of the bodies in the lorry *has not yet entirely been finished*', that indicates that the previously described action (holding a memorial service) should more properly have occurred after the current action (identifying the bodies). The actors in the process of holding a memorial service are even less clearly defined than in the previous representation types; the described processes are agentless passives. This may suggest that, whilst these actions are frowned on, the actors are not (yet). This representation, too, is present whenever secondary relatives are discussed.

Remaining Items

Two sentences remain in which secondary victims are mentioned, but not in a way that fits any of the identified representation types. In one of these, secondary victims are described as having difficulty repatriating the bodies of their relatives due to financial constraints. Aside from this sentence, the experiences of secondary victims, post-identification, receive no further attention. In the other, the mother of one of the presumed victims (pending identification) is reported directly as stating that 'if I were able to go back in time, I would stop him from going there'. Whilst this would feasibly fit with the representation of the 'willing migrant', this sentence also suggests guilt, perhaps complicity, on the part of this relative.

Conclusions and discussion

This study aims to examine the representation of the victims of the 'Essex lorry deaths' in Dutch online-only media reporting on this case, to explore the strategies employed to negotiate the assignation of responsibility to these victims, especially important when the reported crime relates to such legally and ethically sensitive issues as migration and human trafficking. The short answer is that representation mostly sidesteps this question, either by reducing these people to objects of other parties' actions, or by focusing on their deaths without reference to the broader context, which allows a reframing of this case as one of either accidental death or murder. This objectification and dehumanisation of victims is prevalent in newspapers across Europe (Gregoriou et al. 2021). However, occasionally quotes from external parties are included in which these victims are held responsible for their own deaths, either directly or indirectly, by describing the case as one of people-smuggling or migration gone wrong.

Whereas in these online-only articles, this is mainly done using active, material verbs, in European newspapers this is also done through the explicit labelling of these victims as 'migrants' (ibid). As this group of victims, made up of both women and men, teenaged and adult, destination unknown, is difficult to fit into the mould of the ideal victim of human trafficking (Sanford et al. 2016; Farrell and Fahy 2009; Gregoriou and Ras 2018), it is expected that representations either focus on the circumstances directly leading to their deaths, or on their identities as potentially willing migrants, the latter of which leads to negative, victim-blaming portrayals (Brouwer et al. 2017; Gabrielatos and Baker 2008; KhosraviNik 2010). Indeed, the descriptions of these victims as unfortunates potentially attempting to escape desperate circumstances, present in European newspaper reporting (Gregoriou et al. 2021), are absent from the examined reporting, as are explicit discussions on whether these are victims of traffickers or smugglers. Similarly, the reporting on secondary victims, i.e., the relatives, also focuses on the aftermath of the discovery of the victims, again sidestepping complex questions of agency and thereby also the complexities associated with the journey identified by Van Liempt (2011), which renders categorisation of this case as either human trafficking or people

Ilse A. Ras

smuggling meaningless. When sidestepping appears impossible, news outlets maintain an approach best characterised as 'migrant until proven trafficked' or 'guilty until proven innocent'.

These conclusions only apply to a small set of actors in a small set of articles linked to a single case, collected from a small subsection of the Dutch media landscape. This limits the generalisability of these findings: future research would do well to test whether these representations are also found in other (Dutch) media, in relation to other cases. Furthermore, to develop a more complete understanding of the framing of ambiguous smuggling/trafficking cases, representations of other actors, as well as mentioned or implied causes and solutions to these issues, should be examined. Typologies of representations of actors may help in systematising the identification of these representation types, and the current paper aims to contribute to this. However, the reliability of coding in the current study and the validity of the identified representation types are as yet unassessed. Although it fits with findings from earlier research, suggesting that this typology has at least a level of convergent validity, more work is needed to determine the actual usability of this typology in future research.

These representations may, indeed, affect policy and action, as Gonzalez-Pons et al. (2020) show. However, this also requires further empirical examination. It could be useful to compare the types of victim representation this paper identifies with victim representations in the comments to these articles, to illuminate immediate reader responses, but also with victim representations in policy discourses and implementation, as well as broader public understanding and action.

Acknowledgements
Thanks go to Ieke de Vries, PhD, for comments on an earlier draft of this paper, and to Carmen Withag, MSc, for contributing to the list of search terms.

Notes
[1] https://www.ohchr.org/en/instruments-mechanisms/instruments/protocol-prevent-suppress-and-punish-trafficking-persons

[2] https://www.ohchr.org/en/instruments-mechanisms/instruments/protocol-prevent-suppress-and-punish-trafficking-persons

References
Bakker, Piet (2018) De stand van de nieuwsmedia, *Stimuleringsfonds voor de Journalistiek* [Dutch Journalism Fund]. Available online at https://www.svdj.nl/39-online-nieuwsmerken-bereik/, accessed on 1 September 2022

Brouwer, Jelmer, Woude, Maartje van der and Leun, Joanne van der (2017) Framing migration and the process of immigration: A systematic analysis of the media representation of unauthorized immigrants in the Netherlands, *European Journal of Criminology*, Vol. 14, No. 1 pp 100-119

Christie, Nils (1986) The ideal victim, Fattah, Ezzat (ed.) *From crime policy to victim policy*, London, Palgrave Macmillan

Gabrielatos, Costas and Baker, Paul (2008) Fleeing, sneaking, flooding: A corpus analysis of discursive constructions of refugees and asylum seekers in the UK Press 1996-2005, *Journal of English Linguistics*, Vol. 36, No. 1 pp 5-38

Galtung, Johan and Ruge, Mari (1965) The structure of foreign news: The presentation of the Congo, Cuba, and Cyprus crises in four Norwegian newspapers, *Journal of Peace Research*, Vol. 2, No. 1 pp 64-91

Goffman, Erving (1974) *Frame analysis: An essay on the organization of experience*, Cambridge, Harvard University Press

Gonzalez-Pons, Kwynn, Gezinski, Lindsay, Morzenti, Hanna, Hendrix, Elizabeth and Graves, Shelby (2020) Exploring the relationship between domestic minor sex trafficking myths, victim identification, and service provision, *Child Abuse & Neglect*, Vol. 100.

Gregoriou, Christiana, Ras, Ilse and Muždeka, Nina (2021) Journey into hell [...where] migrants froze to death': A critical stylistic analysis of European newspapers' first response to the 2019 Essex Lorry deaths, *Trends in Organized Crime*, Vol. 25 pp 318-337

Hsieh, Hsui-Fang and Shannon, Sarah (2005) Three approaches to qualitative content analysis, *Qualitative Health Research*, Vol. 15, No. 9 pp 1277-1288

Immigration Act 1971 (c.77) London, The Stationery Office

Jeffries, Lesley (2010) *Critical stylistics*, London, Sage

KhosraviNik, Majid (2010) The representation of refugees, asylum seekers and immigrants in British newspapers: A critical discourse analysis, *Journal of Language and Politics*, Vol. 9, No. 1 pp 1-28

Lakoff, George and Johnson, Mark (1980) *Metaphors we live by*, Chicago, Chicago University Press

Lobasz, Jennifer (2009) Beyond border security: Feminist approaches to human trafficking, *Security Studies*, Vol. 18, No. 2 pp 319-344

Modern Slavery Act 2015 (c.30) London, The Stationery Office

Short, Mick (2012) Discourse presentation and speech (and writing, but not thought) summary, *Language and Literature*, Vol. 21, No. 1 pp 18-32

Sobel, Megan (2014) Chronicling a crisis: Media framing of human trafficking in India, Thailand, and the USA, *Asian Journal of Communication*, Vol. 24, No. 4 pp 315-332

UN General Assembly (2000) *Protocol against the smuggling of migrants by land, sea and air, supplementing the United Nations Convention against Transnational Organised Crime*, 15 November. Available online at https://www.refworld.org/docid/479dee062.html, accessed on 31 August 2022

UN General Assembly (2000) *Protocol to prevent, suppress and punish trafficking in persons, especially women and children, supplementing the United Nations Convention against Transnational Organised Crime*, 15 November. Available online at https://www.refworld.org/docid/4720706c0.html, accessed on 31 August 2022

Van Liempt, Ilse (2011) Different geographies and experiences of 'assisted' types of migration: A gendered critique on the distinction between trafficking and smuggling, *Gender, Place and Culture*, Vol. 18, No. 2 pp 179-193

Note on the contributor
Dr Ilse A. Ras works as an Assistant Professor in Criminology at Leiden University. She has previously worked as a researcher at Leeds University Business School and Leeds University School of English and is a co-founder of the Poetics and Linguistics Association Special Interest Group on Crime Writing.

Conflict of interest
No funding was received for the research presented in the paper.

PAPER

Nicholas Beckmann

Murder tales – True crime narratives between fact and fiction: A troubled relationship

True crime narratives come in various medial forms. They all share the same subject, crime – especially murder – but differ with respect to their self-understanding and the medial rulebook they rely on. While seemingly non-fictional, they oscillate between various self-attributions – journalistic or belletristic, truth-driven or mainly entertaining – or an amalgam of these features, which is defined by the troubled relationship of fact and fiction. It is the challenging interplay of contexts which makes true crime narratives a highly interesting field of investigation for transmedial working narratologists. This paper discusses the genre and its distinctive attributes by debating its status between factual-informing and fictional-entertaining narrations, and taking its storytelling methods into focus, where true crime's troubled relationship of fact and fiction primarily evokes questions of (un-)reliability and trustworthiness.

Keywords: true crime, factuality, unreliability, *Serial*, storytelling

Introduction

It is almost trivial to state that stories about murder and manslaughter have been told all along, and they always evoke fascination. Crime stories have been and still are even more interesting when true. Nowadays, true crime is omnipresent; historically speaking it is having a renaissance (Burger 2016: n.p.) especially in streaming shows and podcasts. Columnists ask 'why is true crime popular culture's most wanted?' (Lawson 2015) and wonder what the recent true crime hype may reveal about modern, Western societies of the 21st century. A voyeuristic interest in human abysses and 'sensationalism' (Wiltenburg 2004: 1377), which is certainly undeniable in principle, is not sufficient to explain the success of true crime narratives. This question, however, can only be answered by taking true crime's storytelling into focus.

This paper claims the famous podcast *Serial* revolutionised radio and podcast storytelling by telling a true, serially developing story that builds up and sustains suspense, practises cliffhangers and traces character development (Schelander et al. 2019). Moreover, a transmedial transfer rather than an innovation took place, since the narrative methods in true crime are borrowed (transferred) from serial television storytelling.

The revolutionary aspect consists most likely of the interplay of factual and fictional narration and is founded in the immersive narrative technique, which makes it possible to let listeners participate in the journalistic work of the *Serial* editors, and in the special form of narration that lets the listeners participate in the presenter's thinking and the narration process.

This paper sets out a programme to establish true crime stories as a promising field of research for narratologists. Starting from an informal typological perspective, this paper aims at (firstly) discussing the genre and its distinctive features by (secondly) debating its character between factual-informing and fictional-entertaining narrations. In fact, true crime often does not claim to be omniscient, but rather intends to be as truthful as possible. Especially when true crime stories come across as journalistic narratives, they often imply a firm hypothesis of what happened, a feature which (thirdly) evokes questions of (un-)reliability and trustworthiness.

True crime as genre

True crime stories are by no means a recent invention, although this impression is common, given the increasing popularity of true crime publications in the current popular culture landscape. Burger elaborates on the 'bloody history of the true crime genre' and draws a line back to the 16th century, when 'British authors and printers produced an unprecedented number of publications that reported on capital crimes' (Burger 2016). These pamphlets are not criminal reports in a (modern) journalistic sense, but ballades broaching the issue of the most violent crimes, as Burger points out (ibid).

Nicholas Beckmann

In the history of *modern* true crime stories and their success, there are two peaks: in 1966, Truman Capote's non-fictional novel *In cold blood* establishes the modern literary true crime genre, when re-constructing[1] the gruesome murder of four members of the Clutter family in Kansas, USA. And in 2014, the podcast-show *Serial* reinvents and transfers true crime into the digital age. Countless adaptions followed and are still following.

While fictional crime stories are extensively explored by literary studies and related disciplines, true crime narratives are far less comprehensively explored. To understand true crime as an independent genre, we need to identify what constitutes true crime narratives, what defines differences and/or similarities to fictional crime stories and, finally, answer the question: what are their distinctive features? Yet, regarding the elements of true crime stories, I claim they do *not* differ that much from fictional crime stories. What constitutes a true crime narrative boils down to a simple recipe that is easily perpetuated: we need a crime case, a victim, a perpetrator and an investigating authority. And we need someone who narrates the story.

The narrator is the crucial entity: in the case of true crime stories, the narrator's narrative possibilities are regulated by a *factual pact* (or truth pact), which defines (and defends) the story to the recipients as *truthful*. This so-called factual pact is already communicated by the paratext[2] which claims the story is true crime, thereby laying the foundations on which factual narratives are developed.

An initial proposal for a typology is provided by the film and media scholar Stella Bruzzi, who takes a look at documentary – predominantly film – true crime formats and identifies genre-constituting characteristics (Bruzzi 2016: 278), but thus merely scratches the surface of a much more diverse complexity. Previous attempts to develop true crime as a literary genre (Seltzer 2007) help to understand true crime from a literary-historical perspective. These attempts, however, are still tentative in nature and lack a well-defined empirical and theoretical foundation: the genre developed too rapidly to be adequately captured by the descriptive tools developed for fictional crime literature.

A first attempt to frame true crime theoretically is made by journalist Ian Case Punnett in his book *Toward a theory of true crime narratives: A textual analysis* (Punnett 2018). Punnett undertakes a rather long-winded attempt to break down the factuality pact into typological features, in the course of defining what he calls a true crime code: 'TC = TEL + 4/{JUST, SUB, CRUS, GEO, FOR, VOC, FOLK}' (ibid: 99). Thus, true crime is composed of the obligatory item *teleology*, which ensures that the narrative moves toward factuality or 'toward truth' (ibid: 96). This is completed by at least four of seven further possible items, such as *justice, subversive, crusader, geographic, forensic, vocative* and *folkloric*. However, this provides only a superficial description of how true crime narratives are composed and which content units they may consist of. In the end, his true crime formula sheds only a rather pale light on the subject and appears more like a theoretical corset than a well-founded explication.

When thinking about true crime, these narratives surface in various medial forms. They all share the same subject, namely a crime – preferably murder – but they differ both with respect to their self-conception and the medial playbook they rely on. While they claim to be non-fictional by their very nature, these narratives oscillate between various self-attributions, depending on whether they are driven by journalistic or belletristic, truth-driven or mainly entertaining interests; they may even present a mixture of all of these features. This mixture is, inter alia, defined by the fundamentally troubled relationship of fact and fiction. We must conclude, when facing true crime narratives, that we are confronted with a highly diverse, transmedial genre.

True crime's status between *factual-informing* and *fictional-entertaining intentions*

The podcast show *Serial* is still considered the most important and successful podcast, and it qualifies as a prelude to a real boom of true crime. The tragic story of Hae Min Lee, a high school student from Baltimore County/Maryland, who disappeared on 13 January 1999 without leaving a trace, received considerable attention in 2014 due to the show. This exemplifies how 'narrative work' can generate a reflex on reality, i.e., it triggers resonance outside the narrated world and is taken so seriously in the investigative process that it even (re)initiates the investigations of law enforcement officials.

Serial revolutionised radio and podcast by serialising the story throughout a complete season, building up and sustaining suspense, involving cliff-hangers and tracing character development. This is not only due to well-known podcast storytelling methods, but facilitated by means of modern, fictionalising storytelling methods in serial narrations which help keep the audience on board. It also shows how factual narratives can evoke real-life experience, so-called experientiality (Fludernik 2002: 9).

Additionally, empirical studies show that consumers of true crime publications are not only driven by their wish to come to a better understanding of crimes and a general need for entertainment; they also hope to learn from them for a better self-protection against the risk of becoming victims of criminal assaults (Vicary and Fraley 2010: 82).[3] In Germany this latter effect/intention is described as *Lebensweltbezug* (roughly translating into a concept of 'reference to the own living-world'): the reception of true crime enables the listener, reader or recipient in general to peek into the lives and experiences of others. In turn, this gives the audience the opportunity to identify with the stories (or not).[4] In other words, the narrators succeed in constructing a plot, which can drag the recipients into the story, primarily via the re-construction of characters, their suffering and experiences (Fludernik 2002: 18).

Serial: Homodiegetic storytelling to create experientiality

The main case study for this paper to exemplify the impact of storytelling methods could not be any other – and more suitable regarding the *Erkenntnisinteresse*[5] – than the mother of modern true-crime-storytelling itself: *Serial*.

The concept of storytelling, like the concept of narrativity, is currently booming in many academic disciplines and has, to a certain extent, become a buzzword. Storytelling, understood as a discursive method of telling a story, currently serves as a theoretical concept in the practice of narrative, especially in audiovisual media or in broadcast or podcasting. Storytelling is understood as an act of construction on the one hand and as an act of interpretation on the part of the audience on the other. Accordingly, storytelling does not necessarily mean inventing, but describes a narrative method – a practice of doing – that motivates stories in a certain way and thus creates narrative coherence. It encompasses at the same time aesthetic literary techniques and possibilities of storytelling.

The first episode of the first season welcomes its listeners with a short, but equally sophisticated prelude, followed by an introduction of the narrator and her point of view.

Prelude (Intro):

[Automated voice]

This is a Global-Tel link prepaid call from [Syed:] Adnan Syed, an inmate at a Maryland correctional facility...

[Sarah Koenig]: From This American Life WBEZ Chicago it's *Serial*. One story told week by week. I'm Sarah Koenig. For the last year, I've spent every working day trying to figure out where a high school kid was for an hour after school one day in 1999 – or if you want to get technical about it, and apparently, I do, where a high school kid was for 21 minutes after school one day in 1999. This search sometimes feels undignified on my part. I've had to ask about teenagers' sex lives, where, how often, with whom, about notes they passed in class, about their drug habits, their relationships with their parents.

And I'm not a detective or a private investigator. I'm not even a crime reporter. But, yes, every day this year, I've tried to figure out the alibi of a 17-year-old boy. Before I get into why I've been doing this, I just want to point out something I'd never really thought about before I started working on this story. And that is, it's really hard to account for your time, in a detailed way, I mean (Koenig 2014: 00:00-01:15).

When listening to the first episode of *Serial*, already in this intro the recipients learn several crucial things: (1) someone named Adnan Syed is an inmate at a Maryland correctional facility; (2) in this show he himself will be talking by calling the show's host; (3) the host is Sarah Koenig, a journalist at a big radio station in Chicago; and (4) she worked at least for a year on the case that she narrates. In the first minute and fifteen seconds, the recipients do not learn what happened, but rather who is suspected, or even guilty: the 17-year-old Adnan Syed. This method is obviously used to catch the audience's attention by raising the question: 'What happened here?' It urges the need for finding a solution in order to satisfy previously aroused curiosity; the listeners want to find an answer.

Koenig then moves on by describing Hae Min Lee so that the listeners can construct some kind of mental image of her: 'She was a senior at Woodlawn High School in Baltimore County in Maryland. She was Korean. She was smart, and beautiful, and cheerful, and a great athlete. She played field hockey and lacrosse. And she was responsible' (ibid: 03:38-03:50). Right after the brief introduction, slow and sad, but

Nicholas Beckmann

still suspenseful, music is played. The listeners learn that Lee did not pick up her cousin from kindergarten after school as expected, and that by this moment 'everyone' knew that something was amiss, because – as we also learn – Hae Min Lee was very responsible, and that this kind of alleged unreliability was simply out of character.

Without any further background story, we learn that her body was found about four weeks later. 'The cause of death,' as Koenig tells, 'was manual strangulation, meaning someone did it with their hands' (ibid: 04:16-04:20). Shortly after, Jay Wilds, one of Lee's schoolmates, comes forward and accuses Lee's ex-boyfriend Adnan Syed of strangling her to death out of jealousy. Koenig elaborates that Syed is in prison, but keeps insisting on his innocence (ibid: 04:33).

This dense narrative is well composed: within the first six minutes, the listeners gain all the basic knowledge they need to follow the narration. Meanwhile, the narrative itself raises different questions, points out blanks and leaves the audience curious for more.

What makes *Serial*'s storytelling special is described by Colleen Morrissey as 'both a journalistic and a personal quest to find the truth, revisiting crime scenes, retracing Lee's steps, talking to witnesses, and, most importantly, extensively interviewing Syed himself' (Morrissey 2020: 167). This is actually a crucial observation; one of the most interesting features of true crime is that the author and narrator *can* be the same person. Koenig figures as a homodiegetic narrator, since she is part of her own story about investigating the case. One could even say she is an autodiegetic narrator since she could be understood as the narrator and the main character in her own story. She compares the case to a Shakespeare play:

> I read a few newspaper clips about the case, looked up a few trial records. And on paper, the case was like a Shakespearean mash-up – young lovers from different worlds thwarting their families, secret assignations, jealousy, suspicion and honour besmirched, the villain not a Moor exactly, but a Muslim all the same, and a final act of murderous revenge. And the main stage? A regular old high school across the street from a 7-Eleven (ibid: 05:26-05:52).

According to Martínez and Scheffel, there are six different levels of involvement of the narrator in events, which are located along a spectrum from an uninvolved narrator to the narrating main character, whereby basically two forms of participation of the narrator and the events are identified. First of all, a differentiation is made between: (1) narratives in which the narrator is involved as a character in the story he or she tells (homodiegetic narrator); and (2) narratives in which the narrator is not part of the story (heterodiegetic narrator) (Martínez and Scheffel 2016: 86). This distinction also is understood by the differentiation between the experiencing and the narrating narrator, where the homodiegetic narrator is both experiencing *and* narrating.

Koenig's storytelling allows listeners not only to get pulled into the story but to take part in every single step of the investigation. She shares her private thoughts, her doubts and her opinion on evidence or the prosecutor's timeline. Additionally, Morrissey points out:

> Koenig's intonation *does* have the effect of making her narration sound more spontaneous instead of scripted, which, in turn, creates an air of intimacy with the listener, as though Koenig were ingenuously thinking out loud rather than reading from a script. (Morrissey 2020: 186)

Moreover, it is not only her own storytelling and subjectivity luring the listeners into the story, but also the plot's immersive design, which allows witnesses, friends and family to tell their story and enables them to share their view – they surface as intradiegetic narrators, narrating embedded stories.

All this is as relatable, transparent and as honest as possible. It is not coincidental, but a narrative and composition technique to attest to the truthfulness of the narration. When the narrators incorporate 'historical' documents or (eye-)witness accounts into the narrative, journalists clearly, (1) make use of theory-based practices of historical science and knowledge that enable them to authenticate the story historically. Sending out the respective signals is, therefore, not enough; they must be (2) verified, for example, through publishing the source material on their own website or by simply integrating it into the podcast.

Immersion is established by means of techniques that invigorate the narrative by emphasising the factuality of the narration and the text and also by creating the impression that what is narrated is genuinely present (Dam 2019: 67). Meanwhile, the conception of the season of *Serial* as a coherent narrative and its fabrication of an ominously sombre storyworld (mainly through sound designs) only enhances this immersion effect because its procedures arouse and increase the listener's imagination. Due to these processes, listeners are immersed in the narrative world.

When compared, for instance, with the Netflix show *Night stalker: The hunt for a serial killer*, which not only differs from *Serial* or other narratives because it is not limited to audio, we are also confronted with a totally different narrative approach. While *Serial* comes closer to an investigative journalistic approach searching for the truth, *Night stalker* is more entertaining, aesthetic – especially when taking the images into consideration – and thrilling, since the solution of the case is clear. Furthermore, while in *Serial* Sarah Koenig appears as a distinctive author-narrator, in *Night stalker* the investigators Gil Carillo and Frank Salerno and witnesses appear as intra- or metadiegetic-homodiegetic narrators; there is no distinctive voice-over-narrator. Instead, it is merely the camera and cutting which are narrating the story.

(Un-)reliability and trustworthiness

When narrating factual stories, a theoretical discrepancy emerges that contradicts the expositional claim of true crime narratives, namely to state complex issues and descriptions of events mapping to reality in a truth-functionally way. Propositions in true crimes are claimed to correspond to 'the truth'.

However, as stated at the beginning of this paper, a deeper look into true crime narratives challenges the *paradigm of truth* on various levels, that is, on the levels of researching, reconstructing and re-narrating even when remembering crime. The problematic relationship between fact and fiction in true crime narratives is a core one that needs to theoretical understanding, but it may appear a pseudo-problem when viewed from the outside. Eventually, the paratext true crime already gives the supposedly decisive hint to a true, factual story. A factual narrative is fundamentally constrained by its obligation to the truth pact, even narratively. This is only further exacerbated when journalistic formats are considered, because for all the acceleration of mediated narrative dynamics, there are formal limits to the journalistic true crime narrative: journalism must above all be truthful if it wants to remain credible (Renner and Schupp 2017: 125).

The main difficulty emerging around the term of 'credibility' is implied by Hayden White's famous notion of the *fiction of the factual representation*, a notion originally developed with respect to historical science (White 1978: 122). Narrators cannot *re*construct the criminal case but can only *construct* plausible scenarios based on the information available to them as to how it may have been, and the witnesses can only share *their* perspective. White argues that this makes all historical writing fiction – I am defending the hypothesis that this claim is also valid for true crime. True crime is unreliable given the narrator's position, their access and their perspective. However, true crime as fiction does not mean fictional in a literal sense, but rather it is aesthetic, constructed and narrated.

The fictionality of narration is covered by Koenig's *thinking out loud* storytelling; this specific technique is interpreted as one out of many possible signals of factuality. This technique, as DeMair (2019) and Morrissey (2020) point out, is supported by reality effects (the author prefers the term *factuality signs*) of archival audio such as interrogation or court tapings. The listeners tend to believe the story even more because they 'can' confirm themselves. The audience tends to believe the investigators Carillo and Salerno in the Netflix show since they actually caught the serial killer. All this, of course, is well composed and orchestrated. Factuality signals[6] help confirm the story, thereby making it more trustworthy. It fits into the storyworld and into the character inventory the narrator constructs, but in the end this construction is nothing more than the narrator's interpretation.

Therefore, factual narratives (and true crime narratives in particular) cannot be objective but are always biased. Sarah Koenig opens up about her own perspective and methods, making them accessible and clear to the listeners; for instance, when she describes how she came upon the Syed case and how it sparked her interest. Koenig also claims to have fact-checked every detail she was told. This again generates trust in the audience. The recipients can even fact-check documents or audio on the *Serial* website by themselves. And while *Serial* does not claim omniscience, it aims to be as truthful (and transparent) as possible.

Conclusion

True crime narratives are successful because they seem obliquely to touch on a true crime recipient's surrounding world, that is, from a safe perspective. A general voyeuristic interest in human abysses does not suffice as an explanation for their popularity. Instead, storytelling methods and narrative formats have changed considerably, catalysing true crime stories' pop-

Nicholas Beckmann

ularity. They are modernised, as is seen in the variety of true-crime shows and books which meet the *Zeitgeist* and current story reading habits. At the same time, in the broad field of crime stories, true crime as a genre of its own is well located between fact and fiction.

True crime as a genre is highly diverse and can only be understood transmedially, that is, by considering the complete range of their possible modes of medial representation. While their basic narrative outline does not differ crucially from the outline of purely fictional criminal stories, the factuality pact determines a regulated relationship between the author-narrator and the audience. In other words: the factuality pact is a hard constraint (or filter) on possible, well-formed true crime 'narrative outputs'. The interplay of fictional narrative methods and its aim to narrate a suspenseful and interesting story on the one hand and the use of (by definition: non-fictional) factuality signs on the other, creates a troubled relationship of fact and fiction. Fictional narrative methods and the use of factuality signs mutually interfere, where the very nature of the 'true crime scenario' depends on the legitimising strength of the non-fictional (model/construction of) reality.

The podcast *Serial* shifted boundaries, making formerly opaque barriers more transparent and, thus, decisively shaped the true crime podcast. Journalistic narrations not only allow subjectivity in principle, but also often require the subjectivistic view in order to produce an exciting narrative which is the prerequisite for successfully generating experientiality – experientiality allows recipient immersion into the narrative. The oral mode of presentation does have an impact on the degree of experientiality of the narrative. Depending on the respective narrative culture and tradition, however, the depth of impact of an orally perceived narration differs considerably. Furthermore, within a given tradition/culture of narrating, a fundamental difference is observed in the storytelling approach, that is, in the choice of means of linguistic transmission. This is particularly striking in the comparison of oral text (podcast) and written text.

The scholarly reception to date raises more questions than it is able to answer: Colleen Morrissey describes the *Serial* format as a narrative podcast, which she defines as 'a single story told across multiple episodes, produced either for web-simultaneous or exclusive web release (as opposed to the more one-off structure of interview-based or comedy podcasts)' (Morrissey 2020: 167). Following Morrissey's definition by emphasising the feature of seriality, however, excludes non-serial podcast formats from consideration by classifying them as non-narrative. This is counter-intuitive and proves Morrisey's definition as too powerful, since podcasts that do not narrate serially are still narrative in nature.

While this paper only points out some questions and problems, a comprehensive analysis of true crime could contribute to a better understanding of how true crime works on a narrative level. A better understanding of its specific 'narrative dynamics' could also contribute to a better understanding of its success in popular culture.

Notes

[1] In the following the author prefers speaking of re-construction rather than reconstruction, because one cannot reconstruct events of the past in every detail. The true-crime author simply presents their perspective when narrating the case. Ideally, they make themselves visible as narrators in order to give readers and/or recipients the space to construct a story by themselves

[2] Paratexts are an essential part of the narrative and textual architecture. We encounter paratextual elements when dealing with any kind of text: the author uses a broad concept of text and, therefore, also considers medial narratives as texts and they provide basic information about content and author. They reveal a genre classification, they create order and structure, they provide orientation markers, they complement, comment on, or update the main text and, ideally, they facilitate the reception of the text. Their function, however, is by no means reduced to these parameters. Rather, they make the comprehensive reception of the text possible in the first place

[3] In their study, Vicary and Fraley interestingly conclude that 'women consider true crime books more appealing when the victims are female [which] supports the notion that women may be attracted to these books because of the potential life-saving knowledge gained from reading them' (Vicary and Fraley 2010: 85). This conclusion, however, is speculative in nature

[4] Current true crime formats make use of modern communication channels. While *Serial* uses its website to provide additional information and material, today's podcasts (e.g. *Crime junkie*) use social media to reach out to their audience or even organise live events

[5] For lack of a better term, the author apologises using *Erkenntnisinteresse* to express what roughly translates into scientific interest

[6] Factuality signs are textual or visual markers or even source material, justifying or ensuring the story just as mentioned above (e.g. court or interrogation tapes or as in *Night stalker* original footage of the crime scene or the perpetrator)

References

Bruzzi, Stella (2016) Making a genre: The case of the contemporary true crime documentary, *Law and Humanities*, Vol. 10, No. 2 pp 249-280

Burger, Pamela (2016) The bloody history of the true crime genre, *JSTOR Daily*. Available online at https://daily.jstor.org/bloody-history-of-true-crime-genre/, accessed on 23 August 2022

Dam, Beatrix van (2019) Belegen und beleben? Geschichtserfahrung und Metahistoriographie in populären Geschichtserzählungen der Gegenwart [Evidencing and enlivening? Historical experience and metahistoriography in popular contemporary historical narratives], Fulda, D. and Jaeger, S. (eds) *Romanhaftes Erzählen von Geschichte*, Berlin, Boston, De Gruyter pp 57-80

DeMair, Jillian (2019) Sounds authentic: The acoustic construction of *Serial*'s storyworld, McCracken, E. (ed.) *The Serial podcast and storytelling in the digital age*, New York, London, Routledge pp 24-38

Fludernik, Monika (2002) *Towards a 'natural' narratology*, London, Routledge

Lawson, Mark (2015) Serial thrillers: Why true crime is popular culture's most wanted, *Guardian*, 12 December. Available online at http://www.theguardian.com/culture/2015/dec/12/serial-thrillers-why-true-is-popular-cultures-most-wanted, accessed on 29 August 2022

Martínez, Matías and Scheffel, Michael (2016) *Einführung in die Erzähltheorie* [*Introduction to narrative theory*], Vol. 10, Munich, C. H. Beck, revised edition

Morrissey, Colleen (2020) 'The grief manual': Fact, fiction, and narrative podcasts, Breitenwischer, D., Häger, H.-M. and Menninger, J. (eds) (2020) *Faktuales und fiktionales Erzählen II* [*Factual and fictional narrating II*], Würzburg, Ergon pp 167-192

Koenig, Sarah (2014) The alibi, Episode 1, *Serial*. Available online at https://serialpodcast.org/season-one/1/the-alibi, accessed on 29 August 2022

Punnett, Ian Case (2018) *Toward a theory of true crime narratives: A textual analysis*, Abingdon, Routledge

Renner, Karl Nikolaus and Schupp, Katja (2017) Journalismus, Martínez, M. (ed.) *Erzählen*, Stuttgart, J. B. Metzler pp 122-132

Schelander, Esther et al. (2019) Podcasting in Deutschland: Storytelling fünf Jahre nach *Serial*, *Hörspiel und feature* [Podcasting in Germany. Storytelling five years after *Serial*]. Available online at https://www.deutschlandfunkkultur.de/podcasting-in-deutschland-storytelling-fuenf-jahre-nach.3688.de.html?dram:article_id=465057, accessed on 29 August 2022

Seltzer, Mark (2007) *True crime: Observations on violence and modernity*, New York, Routledge

Vicary, Amanda M. and Fraley, R. Chris (2010) Captured by true crime: Why are women drawn to tales of rape, murder, and serial killers?, *Social Psychological and Personality Science*, Vol. 1, No. 1 pp 81-86

White, Hayden (1978) *Tropics of discourse: Essays in cultural criticism*, Baltimore, Johns Hopkins University Press

Wiltenburg, Joy (2004) True crime: The origins of modern sensationalism, *The American Historical Review*, Vol. 109, No. 5 pp 1377-1404

Note on the contributor

Nicholas Beckmann is a German historian and literary scholar. He primarily works in narrative theory and is interested in interdisciplinary and cultural studies issues. His work focuses on the relationship between factuality and fictionality in narrative texts, immersion and (trans-)medial narrative forms.

Conflict of interest

The author did not receive any funding for the research and publication.

PAPER

Kelli S. Boling

'I'm not a journalist. I don't think that I necessarily fall under the same rules that they do': Journalistic ethics in true crime podcast production

Crime junkie, *widely regarded as the most popular true crime podcast, is accused of repeated plagiarism and potential intellectual property infringement. These claims are well-documented, yet the podcast remains highly successful. This study examines the ethical implications of plagiarism in an unregulated industry through the lens of media coverage, an interview with the host of* Crime junkie, *and responses from audience and industry peers. I argue that the future of the true crime genre and podcast media could be impacted by how well-known podcasts are held responsible (or not) for their actions.*

Keywords: podcasts, true crime, journalism, Crime junkie, Ashley Flowers, ethics

Introduction
In December 2017, Ashley Flowers and Brit Prawat launched Crime junkie, a true crime podcast that typically covers a different case each week (Flowers and Prawat 2017-present; Swan 2019). Within 15 months, it was named one of the top true crime podcasts by Rolling Stone and highly ranked on both Spotify and iTunes (Barcella 2018). By month 18, it was counting downloads by the millions (Medium 2019). Four years post-launch, it regularly ranks in the top three of all podcasts on iTunes (Apple Podcasts 2021).

In August 2019, four sources accused Flowers of plagiarism (Inside Radio 2019; Ludlow 2019; Quah 2019; Taylor and Hauser 2019; Wren 2019). Described as one of the top five plagiarism and attribution cases of 2019, the story was covered by large media outlets across the US (Smith 2020). In an interview just two weeks earlier, Flowers says: 'I'm not a journalist. I don't think that I necessarily fall under the same rules that they do' (Boling 2020). However, the ensuing media coverage and audience response to plagiarism claims implies otherwise (Quah 2019; Taylor and Hauser 2019; Wren 2019). In the aftermath of these plagiarism accusations, Flowers claims to have changed her practices to align more closely with journalistic ethics and begun regularly citing sources in the podcast and show notes (Ganz 2021).

However, in 2022, Flowers faced other accusations. Her new podcast, The deck, which uses cold case playing cards to cover crimes, is strikingly similar to Dealing justice, a podcast launched in 2020 (Cridland 2022). Not only is it similar, but sources who worked with Dealing justice informed Flowers of the podcast's existence before her launch of The deck, raising additional ethical concerns (Cridland 2022).

Her podcast network, Audiochuck, is now home to 16 different podcasts, and she has 'tens of thousands of members' in her fan club, paying $5 to $20 per month (Rosman 2022). She has also written a novel, released in August 2022, featuring a hometown journalist trying to solve two local cases (Penguin Random House). While Flowers has launched a non-profit offering funding for genetic testing in cold cases (Marks 2021), she is also clear that she is running a for-profit business (Rosman 2022). She adamantly denies she is a journalist, and she is vocal regarding her goals for the future of her true crime podcast empire (ibid).

This study examines the ethical tension between the lack of podcast governance and the audience's assumption that podcasts adhere to the same standards as traditional media outlets (Inside Radio 2020). Examining the Society of Professional Journalists' (SPJ) code of ethics (2014) alongside an interview with Flowers, media coverage of the plagiarism accusations, and audience/peer response, I discuss the contrast between her beliefs regarding journalistic ethics and how the industry is attempting to hold her to the journalistic standards which she argues do not apply.

Journalistic norms and true crime podcasts
The concept of objectivity in journalism stems from the idea that journalists need to be seen as neutral and, if they remain objective, they

can protect themselves from criticism (Deuze 2005; Tuchman 1972). While the SPJ code of ethics does not explicitly use the word 'objective', it offers clear guidance on integrity and attribution in the preamble, 'An ethical journalist acts with integrity' (SPJ code of ethics 2014). As a point of clarity in the tenet of 'seek truth and report it', the code states: 'Never plagiarize. Always attribute' (ibid).

The plagiarism claims against *Crime junkie* are two-fold. First, it did not consistently cite the journalistic sources that covered the cases (Ludlow 2019); often, it used what those journalists wrote verbatim. Second, it copied other true crime podcasts verbatim (Ludlow 2019). While removing the episodes and citing the journalistic sources addresses the first issue (but does not fully correct it), it does not address the second. To clarify, citing a source but not identifying verbatim statements from that source as belonging to them is still plagiarism. In this situation with *Crime junkie*, it cites the sources on its website but the audio of the podcast is not changed to indicate verbatim passages taken from media coverage. In addition, it does not cite the other podcasters quoted verbatim or change the audio in those episodes (Ludlow 2019).

In our ever-changing media environment, podcasters often have a variety of roles. While some true crime podcasts are produced by journalists working for traditional media outlets, others are produced by lawyers working for the defence, police detectives, fans of the genre and those looking to capitalise on a growing genre and medium. In the journalism industry, there are clear guiding principles. However, the podcast industry is unregulated and unmanaged. While some true crime podcasters adhere to journalistic ethics, there is no regulatory oversight ensuring compliance.

In 2021, Edison Research published a study showing that 41 per cent of US residents 12-years-old and older listened to a podcast in the last month. Those identifying as podcast listeners report consuming an average of eight episodes per week. This is a substantial increase on 2008, when Edison reported only 9 percent had done so, suggesting increasing interest in the medium (Edison Research 2021). Not only has the medium grown significantly, but so has its potential for revenue. True crime is now the third most popular podcast genre in the United States and sixth in total advertising revenue (Statista 2020).

While there is no single definition of true crime, prior research describes the genre as focusing on a truthful depiction of real cases with the goal of entertaining audiences, often reflecting societal concerns (Horeck 2019; Punnett 2018). Research also criticises the genre for capitalising on and re-victimising survivors and/or the families of victims (Yardley et al. 2019), and for shining light on societal injustices but leaving the causes perpetuating abuse largely unchallenged (Slakoff 2021; Yardley et al. 2019). The genre is also criticised widely by mass media for perpetuating interest in criminal acts and those who cause harm (Mallett 2019; Sharma 2020). Since many true crime podcasts are produced by independent podcasters without regulatory oversight or journalistic training, it is also called the 'wild wild west' of media (Gumble 2021).

Methodology

This case study in true crime podcast ethics requires examination from three different angles: an interview with Ashley Flowers; an analysis of *Crime junkie* media coverage; and an analysis of the response to the plagiarism allegations from both the media and a plagiarism claimant discussion between three true crime podcasters in 2019.

During a 35-minute interview with Flowers on 6 August 2019, we discussed the true crime podcast industry. News coverage of *Crime junkie* was collected on 28 March 2022 using the Nexis Uni database and search terms 'Ashley Flowers' or 'Crime junkie', 'Ashley Flowers and plagiarism', 'Crime junkie and plagiarism', and 'Crime junkie or plagiarism'. A total of 752 articles were identified within a date range of 2017-2022, spanning the year that *Crime junkie* launched and concluding after the most recent plagiarism allegations. After removing duplicates and irrelevant articles, 25 were selected for analysis.

Audience response was gathered through several Reddit threads, including r/TrueCrimePodcasts, r/TrueCrime, r/podcasts, and r/CrimeJunkiePodcast. The r/CrimeJunkiePodcast Reddit thread keeps a pinned post with coverage about the plagiarism scandals at the top of the page for those searching for information. A total of 18 relevant Reddit threads were identified, and comments copied from Reddit into a new document with user identities removed for analysis. True crime podcaster response was obtained by analysing an episode of *Let's taco 'bout true crime* where the host, Esther Ludlow, interviews Steven Pacheco from *Trace evidence* and Robin Warder from *The trail went cold*

Kelli S. Boling

(Ludlow 2019). All three podcasters claim that Flowers plagiarised their work.

The interview, news coverage, Reddit threads and podcast episodes were all transcribed for analysis and examined using Saldaña's (2021 [2012]) qualitative coding methods. For this study, I look at how Ashley Flowers is described as a podcaster and an entrepreneur. I also am interested in how the plagiarism allegations are addressed from all three angles. The first round of coding was used to identify themes and explore the accusations of plagiarism, while the second round of coding adds clarity and context to the themes for analysis.

'I'm not a journalist'
In my interview with Ashley Flowers, before the plagiarism claims, we discussed the true crime podcast industry, how she sees her role in the industry and what she wishes for the future of the medium and genre. She describes journalism as being credible and based on research while describing herself as a professional storyteller, entrepreneur and victim advocate. She is also clear regarding her goals in launching the podcast, saying: 'When I launched the podcast, the goal was for me to make it a full-time job.' She argues that full-time employment is necessary because 'It takes a lot of time to research and tell the stories responsibly.'

She repeatedly mentions that she depends on investigative journalists to compile her episodes, describing journalism ethics in a way that sounds aspirational, yet unattainable, for true crime podcasters, saying:

> I want to make sure that everything we talk about has been reported somewhere else, has been reported a couple of times, so that way I know it's been verified and that just kind of keeps us on the up and up legally.

She continues: 'Again, we're not investigative journalists. So, the point of our show is to compile all of this research, news, articles and documentaries, and kind of put it into one digestible 30 or 40-minute story.'

Positioning herself as less than a journalist yet dependent on responsible journalism essentially absolves her from the ethical standards of reporting on a case and the legal implications of any inaccuracies in reporting. She says: 'When I think of true crime podcasters, I would say the majority of us are just like me. We're armchair detectives at home. We have no real-world experience. We're not investigators.'

Since she is 'not an investigator', Flowers also feels that impartiality and objectivity are not required. When asked how she sees the role of objectivity in true crime podcasts, she answers:

> I don't know that I do. I'm not a journalist and I think that maybe that's the difference. It's hard for me to be very objective because I do tend to feel one way or another when I tell a story.

She positions this lack of objectivity in a way that makes her an honorable advocate for the cases she covers, saying: 'I'm not a journalist. I don't think that I necessarily fall under all the same rules that they do. I'm here to tell a story and to make my audience care about the story that I'm telling.'

Taken in a literal sense, that statement implies that journalists are not storytellers, and they do not seek audience empathy for the issues and cases they cover. While Flowers does not explicitly state that, her continued description of herself as a storyteller and 'not a journalist' demonstrates that she sees a distinction between the two. She positions herself firmly as a storyteller, which she believes is a safe position if you do not want to end up in legal trouble regarding the media you produce.

'Building an audio empire'
Media coverage on *Crime junkie* and Ashley Flowers focuses primarily on the launch of her non-profit 'audio empire' and its success, with little coverage of plagiarism claims. Only three major news outlets cover the plagiarism scandal explicitly: *Variety*, *Buzzfeed*, and *The New York Times* (McNeal 2019; Spangler 2019, Taylor and Hauser 2019). While the *Buzzfeed* article is mostly duplicative, *Variety* and *The New York Times* offer distinct perspectives but do not directly condemn *Crime junkie* for the plagiarism claims.

The *Variety* article details the accusations and publishes the provided responses from *Crime junkie*, which notably do not include an apology, describing their research process as '… thorough, rigid, and exhaustive' (Spangler 2019). *Variety* argues: 'Those in the true-crime podcast world say plagiarism is rampant', essentially absolving *Crime junkie* from plagiarism claims because they are not the only podcast plagiarising. While toning down the severity of the plagiarism accusations, *Variety* also discusses Flowers's success as an entrepreneur, mentioning rumours of a *Crime junkie* TV adaptation and the success of her live shows.

There is also a brief mention of an incident where Flowers gains access to case documents that journalists were denied via FOIA [Freedom of Information Act] request, raising other ethical concerns. The *Variety* article details the ethical concerns but frames the situation in the context of Flowers's success and concerns over the industry. There is no mention of the seriousness of plagiarism nor direct condemnation for plagiarising.

The New York Times covers many of the same details as the *Variety* article, adding two additional sources that further tone down the plagiarism accusations (Taylor and Hauser 2019). The first is by David Bailey, the managing editor of the *Arkansas Democrat-Gazette* that published the 2003 series by Cathy Frye, *Crime junkie's* initial plagiarism claimant. Bailey responded via email, saying that Frye is a 'former reporter' at the *Gazette* and that the paper was aware of the issue. He says that the issue is 'effectively rendered moot' because the episode is removed from the website (the episode was removed initially and later reposted with credit to Frye, but the verbatim audio was unchanged).

While Cathy Frye threatened legal action via the lawyers for her former employer, the managing editor appears to have no real concern about the issue. Another claimant, Esther Ludlow, host of the *Once upon a crime* podcast, also appears in *The New York Times*'s coverage discussing plagiarism allegations over an episode from 2018. Ludlow mentions frustration with the situation but is quoted as saying: 'If it gets addressed and it gets corrected in some way, that's kind of good enough for me.' While the article by *The New York Times* covers the accusations, it also demonstrates that none of the claimants are actively pursuing legal action, diminishing the severity of the situation.

The most in-depth and critical article was written and published three months after the plagiarism accusations by Adam Wren at *Indianapolis Monthly* (the city where *Crime junkie* is based) (2019). Wren's article goes into excruciating detail about the charges and what it means for the true crime podcast industry. Addressing the idea that plagiarism is unpunished because the '... podcast ecosystem' is still considered a 'Digital Wild West'. He defines the DWW as:

> ... the requisite gray-area fuzziness and lack of governance around standards of ethical publishing that comes from its relative DWW newness, the prominence of the true crime podcast genre within that gray area and, to some extent, the ramifications of certain podcasts being able to achieve popularity and success while operating deep within that fuzziness.

Wren is the only journalist to publish the portion of Cathy Frye's accusation that calls into question not just the plagiarism but the ethics and integrity of the podcast:

> You said in one of your podcasts that you share these stories in order to reignite interest in old cases. Bullshit. Kacie's murder was solved. Her killer is dead. What you did was simply gratuitous. It served no purpose whatsoever except to serve as 'entertainment' for your audience and as a moneymaker for your podcasts.

This added context demonstrates that this claim of plagiarism is not for altruistic purposes but for capitalistic gains. Wren also attended a *Crime junkie* live show for the article. At the show, Flowers and her co-host Prawat cover the case of a young girl who went missing from Tucson, Arizona, in 2012. At the time of the show, the case was still pending, and a convicted sex offender who had the young girl's sweatshirt buried in his backyard was charged with her murder and facing trial. Flowers and Prawat played the 911 tape for the audience, intentionally drawing suspicions that the father in the call is too nonchalant. According to Wren, Flowers and Prawat lead the audience down a path of suspicion toward the father and never correct their assumptions. Wren concludes:

> Before the tour is over, the six-year-old girl from Tucson will be stalked, kidnapped, and murdered and her father falsely implicated 15 times. In 2019 – even in the face of credible allegations of plagiarism, exploitation, and corrupt storytelling – it's not illegal to turn a podcast about horrific murders and unsolved abductions into a business. But maybe it's a crime.

Flowers is quoted as saying:

> I mean, we genuinely care about the people we're talking about. We never want to forget that every week we're talking about a real event in someone's life that happened, and it was the worst thing that's ever happened in their life.

While the *Variety* and *The New York Times* articles quote Ben Cave, head of Apple Podcasts, by saying that Ms Flowers had 'built one of the

Kelli S. Boling

most successful podcast businesses of all time, completely independently', the *Indianapolis Monthly* article shows the dark side of the true crime industry by focusing on the capitalistic motives of a popular genre (Spangler 2019; Taylor and Hauser 2019; Wren 2019).

True crime discussion on Reddit
The true crime fan discussion on Reddit explores four main topics: the definition of plagiarism and intellectual property theft; proper punishment for these actions; shock that they did not know the details; and the search for other true crime podcast alternatives.

While debating the definition of plagiarism, commenters also question the definition of journalism, and ask who will hold *Crime junkie* accountable. Comments describe the situation as 'plagiarism adjacent', 'sketchy' and 'unethical; she sucks'. One commenter writes: 'Unless Flowers is checked by any of her contemporaries with any clout, nothing will happen.' Another commenter compares the situation to a schoolyard disagreement, writing: 'As far as I know, no one threatened to sue, it was all about "Hey, you stole that from me, I'm telling!" And *Cj* was like "… Ok, and who are you? Heh", took their posts down, and pretty much denied, denied, denied.'

Many commenters are also shocked that they had not heard about the situation in the media or through other podcasts. They describe the plagiarism as calculating and deceptive and blame Ashley Flowers directly. One commenter describes the response as shrewd public relations:

> Ashley Flowers does branding really freaking well and is an engaging storyteller with how she presents a story (tone, inflections, not spoiling the ending early in the episode). Also, from a PR standpoint, they handled the scandal pretty shrewdly overall. I feel like most of their listeners aren't even aware of the extent of the plagiarism that happened. Most of their fans, I talk to feel like it was an unintentional accident, if they are even aware it went on at all.

Several question how *Crime junkie* remains popular in the face of these allegations. One writes: 'I do NOT understand how she continues to receive awards and still be ranked as one of the best podcasts.' Another writes: 'It really is a shame that such an amoral douchebag like AF has had so much success.' Others question the ranking of podcast platforms, writing:

'Clearly Apple Podcast charts are not actually representative because we all fucking hate plagiarism junkie and they are consistently #1. Is there anywhere that shows actual popularity numbers and real reviews?'

There is also general shock that there is no real punishment for plagiarism in podcasting. One commenter writes: 'Until there are standards/ law catches up to podcasting, this type of issue will continue to come up. I'm sure *Crime junkie* is not alone here – they're just big enough that they actually got caught for it.' Another commenter blames the medium for not establishing proper oversight:

> Unfortunately, I think the platforms are heavily resisting regulation. Podcast platforms like iHeartRadio go ahead and comply with broadcast media regulations. But technically, the medium is not completely regulated as its own entity. So there are some wormholes the greedy and crooked are using to scoot around copyright type law … The laws will catch up. And this sort of thing will be much harder to pull off. The listeners won't be the ones pointing it out. The regulatory bodies will be licensing and handing out fines.

Almost every thread, after discussing the issue, the definition of journalism and plagiarism, and what can or cannot be done to make sure it does not happen again, then searches for *Crime junkie* alternatives that do not plagiarise. Interestingly, most of the recommendations are based on the format of *Crime junkie*, two people reviewing a different crime each week based on work produced by seasoned journalists.

'Do I feel vindicated? No'
The industry peers who discussed the plagiarism allegations on the *Let's taco 'bout true crime podcast* are three of the podcasters with claims of plagiarism, and the only three quoted in national media outlets: Esther Ludlow, Steven Pacheco and Robin Warder (Ludlow 2019). In this 90-minute podcast, they cover the allegations in detail, how it impacted them personally and the damage it has done to the true crime podcast industry (Ludlow 2019).

Each podcaster explains how they learned of the plagiarism and the process they went through to verify that they were plagiarised. They describe their emotions as 'surreal' when they began their initial research. Pacheco says: '… the deeper I went into the episode, the more I was starting to find it would stop going from close to verbatim' (Ludlow 2019). The claim that the plagiarism was 'verbatim' is common for all three podcasters, but it went beyond that. Pacheco describes how reading his script verbatim is obvious because he had 'a very particular way' of speaking on that show, and it is not how he speaks when not reading off a script. They also describe mental and physical reactions to the plagiarism. Ludlow (2019) says:

> I'm sitting there, my heart is beating so hard to … hear my words that I spent so much time and energy, you know, researching and writing … coming out of somebody else's mouth. … I was truly shocked. And it really did affect me, physically, which I didn't expect.

Pacheco describes the mental impact:

> For me, it was just sort of a depression I kind of entered after it, because I realised, here's somebody taking work that I've done, they're gonna get a ton more listens … people will accuse me of taking from them (Ludlow 2019).

One key element they wanted to clarify is that the plagiarism is not a one-time event or a mistake. Pacheco says: 'I have found so many similarities across so many episodes at this point that I was able to write up a single-spaced 14-page document of just lines that are plagiarized' (Ludlow 2019). Ludlow followed that up by describing it as a 'pattern of behaviour'. Warder reiterates that when his work was read out: '… it was clear that they hadn't done much research or written their own script.'

While these podcasters experienced plagiarism on a personal level, they are also concerned with the impact on the industry. At one point during the episode, Ludlow reads a statement from Cathy Frye,

> Do I feel vindicated? No … the *Crime junkie* podcast did not apologise or acknowledge that they haven't been citing sources, or crediting journalists or their fellow podcasters. Instead, they claimed that their source material could no longer be found, contending that this is why they were suddenly, and in secrecy, deleting episodes from their website. Their explanation is clearly untrue as my series remains on the *Arkansas-Democrat*.

Ludlow defines plagiarism, citing Merriam-Webster, as 'to steal and pass off the ideas or words of another as one's own' (2019), arguing that this is not just theft of ideas but is also presenting those ideas as your own. Ludlow, Pacheco and Warder voice frustration with both the industry and the audience while discussing the lack of repercussions. Pacheco says: 'It just seems that a lot of *Crime junkie's* fans either don't understand or they don't care' (Ludlow 2019). The frustration stems from the idea that *Crime junkie* did not experience a decrease in its audience, and there is no one to hold it accountable. Warder describes his frustration by saying: 'I can imagine how this would have such a negative effect on podcasters out there and discourage them, especially since there don't seem to be any negative consequences for what they did' (ibid).

The consequences that these podcasters and the audience are seeking are simple – apologise and stop plagiarising. Warden says simply: 'Just do it the right way, don't "regurgitate" someone else's work' (Ludlow 2019). Ludlow goes into more detail:

> If they really just put out a really sincere apology or statement and said, 'Wow, we blew it,' you know, we should have done this, or we weren't aware or whatever they want to say, but to really take ownership and take responsibility that would have gone a long way, I think, to making us all look a little better or feel like … that isn't typical, that isn't normal.

Warden also points out the good that could have come out of a sincere apology, saying:

> I'm not so much mad, but disappointed, because *Crime junkie* is capable of great things like they recently did an episode where they raised a lot of money for the DNA Doe Project. And the reason this was possible is because they have such a large listener base who trusted them and were willing to donate money because of this … they have this large audience now; why not do it for good, like don't just use it to regurgitate other people's material.

Pacheco concludes by reiterating the simplicity of the solution: 'Just, you know, cite your sources and be respectful to the people you got it from maybe once in a while' (ibid).

Discussion

The true crime podcast industry is popular, profitable and growing. Plagiarising other podcasters and journalists in order to produce the most popular and profitable podcast not only lowers the bar for all true crime podcasters but diminishes the good that can come from this industry

Kelli S. Boling

(Ludlow 2019). This paper addresses the ethics of producing a true crime podcast by examining a plagiarism scandal within the industry. However, the larger question is how to set the bar high for everyone so that this medium and this genre are not considered the lowest common denominator in media (Clausen and Sikjær 2021; Flanagin 2016).

Tanya Horeck, author of *Justice on demand: True crime in the digital streaming era*, writes: 'At their best, true-crime podcasts ask us to think critically about crime as a systemic social problem ... At their worst, they stir up emotions for the sake of it' (Seale 2019). If *Crime junkie* was produced by trained journalists, they would likely lose their job and their reputations if they were caught plagiarising to this extent. By positioning herself as 'not a journalist', Flowers is not only able to commit regular, documented plagiarism, but she continues to run a multi-million-dollar profitable business. Her ethics, motives, rankings and success are brought into question, but her podcast continues to top the charts, and her peers are left frustrated and disappointed with no clear recourse.

NPR's Brooke Gladstone argues that 'transparency is the new objectivity' for journalists (England and Speir n.d.). While Flowers is adamant that she is not a journalist, that does not recuse her from moral obligations in storytelling. Transparency in citing sources and acknowledging the work of others builds community within the true crime podcast industry and generates a more positive image of the industry to others. Audiochuck is now a team of professionals producing multiple podcasts, generating income through advertising and winning national awards. Its success is inspiring for other podcasters and it is using its fame to help others with its non-profit organisation. However, it claims to be amateur, with no accountability to the media industry or the cases it covers.

Revisiting the SPJ code of ethics, the main tenets are: 'seek truth and report it,' 'minimize harm,' 'act independently,' and 'be accountable and transparent' (2014). Arguably, in this situation, *Crime junkie* absolves itself from these tenets, and in doing so, openly violates the ethical core of journalism. If the podcasting community was built on the ethical standards of traditional media outlets, trust in the genre and medium could impact crime journalism as a whole and raise societal awareness of criminal justice issues. By classifying itself as entertainment, the ethical bar is lowered, and the need for morality is essentially erased.

According to Wren (2019), as a non-journalist storyteller, Flowers is still responsible for accuracy and truth. He argues: 'And those are just the basic virtues – great storytellers put things in context, give agency to the voiceless, and approach their subject matter with both fervor and empathy.' This raises issues for podcasting as an industry outside of the true crime genre – with no clear oversight or industry standards, what does the future hold for this new media? Who should hold podcasters accountable for the media they produce, and how does the audience know which podcasts are operating in an ethical manner? With no clear answer to these questions, the industry and the audience are left waiting for a leader. If *Crime junkie* is that leader, will the industry follow? Will the industry suffer?

Limitations and future research

This paper is a case study of a plagiarism scandal that impacts the true crime podcast industry and highlights ethical considerations in true crime podcasting. It is not meant to be generalisable to the podcast industry as a whole or the true crime genre. Flowers has not spoken directly to the media regarding the plagiarism accusations, but a more recent interview with her could provide greater depth. Using Reddit as the sole source of audience feedback is limiting to those in the audience on Reddit. A survey or interviews with audience members could offer additional insight into how the audience has interpreted these plagiarism claims.

References

Apple Podcasts – United States of America – True Crime (2021) *Chartable*. Available online at https://chartable.com/charts/itunes/us-true-crime-podcasts, accessed on 24 July 2022

Barcella, Laura (2018) Best true-crime podcasts of 2018, *Rolling Stone*, 31 December. Available online at https://www.rollingstone.com/culture/culture-features/best-true-crime-podcasts-of-2018-773359/, accessed on 22 March 2022

Boling, Kelli S. (2020) Fundamentally different stories that matter: True crime podcasts and the domestic violence survivors in their audiences, PhD thesis. Available online at https://scholarcommons.sc.edu/etd/5959, accessed on 24 July 2022

Clausen, Line Seistrup and Sikjær, Stine Ausum (2021) When podcast met true crime: A genre-medium coevolutionary love story, *Leviathan: Interdisciplinary Journal in English*, Vol. 7 pp 139-214

DePompei, Elizabeth (2019) Indianapolis-based true crime podcast pulls several episodes after plagiarism accusations, *IndyStar*, 21 August. Available online at https://www.indystar.com/story/news/2019/08/21/crime-junkie-plagiarism-accusations-episodes-pulled/2062906001/, accessed on 22 March 2022

Deuze, Mark (2005) What is journalism? Professional identity and ideology of journalists reconsidered, *Journalism*, Vol. 6, No. 4 pp 442-464

England, Natalie and Speir, Marc (n.d) Transparency is the new objectivity, *Moody College of Communication*. Available online at https://moody.utexas.edu/news/transparency-new-objectivity, accessed on 12 August 2022

Flanagin, Jake (2016) How 'true crime' went from guilty pleasure to high culture, *Quartz*, 5 January. Available online at https://qz.com/583998/how-true-crime-went-from-guilty-pleasure-to-high-culture/, accessed on 1 August 2022

Flowers, Ashley and Prawat, Brit (Hosts) (2017-present) *Crime junkie*, audio podcast, *Audiochuck*. Available online at https://crimejunkiepodcast.com/

Ganz, Jami (2021) *Crime junkie* host Ashley Flowers lights a fire under cold cases with new non-profit, *New York Daily News*, 26 September. Available online at https://www.nydailynews.com/snyde/ny-season-of-justice-20210926-uxrqe44gbfa2fmkp245iwgpm3e-story.html, accessed on 22 March 2022

Gumble, Daniel (2021) 'The wild west of media': Stephanie Okupniak on 'A life lived' and the art of podcasting, *Audio Media International*, 28 January. Available online at https://audiomediainternational.com/the-wild-west-of-media-stephanie-okupniak-on-a-life-lived-and-the-art-of-podcasting/, accessed on 24 March 2022

Horeck, Tanya (2019) *Justice on demand: True crime in the digital streaming era*, Detroit, Wayne State University Press

Inside Radio (2019) Arkansas newspaper threatens legal action against *Crime junkie*, 3 September. Available online at http://www.insideradio.com/podcastnewsdaily/arkansas-newspaper-threatens-legal-action-against-crime-junkie/article_f9511906-ce68-11e9-87ab-a7ba08456c8d.html, accessed on 22 March 2022

Inside Radio (2020) Podcasts are a growing news source, media monitors survey shows. Available online at https://www.insideradio.com/podcastnewsdaily/podcasts-are-a-growing-news-source-media-monitors-survey-shows/article_50c300a6-e7bc-11ea-b8dd-2328f848af06.html, accessed on 11 September 2022

Ludlow, Esther A. (Host) (2019) *Let's taco 'bout true crime* the *Crime junkie* plagiarism scandal, audio podcast, *Let's taco 'bout true crime*, 27 August. Available online at https://tacobouttruecrime.libsyn.com/bonus-episode-lets-taco-bout-the-crime-junkie-plagiarism-scandal, accessed on 24 July 2022

Mallett, Xanthe (2019) Glamorising violent offenders with true crime shows and podcasts needs to stop, *The Conversation*, 16 August. Available online at https://theconversation.com/glamorising-violent-offenders-with-true-crime-shows-and-podcasts-needs-to-stop-121806, accessed on 24 July 2022

Marks, Andrea (2021) Podcaster Ashley Flowers launches non-profit to fund DNA testing in cold cases, *Rolling Stone*, 15 July. Available online at https://www.rollingstone.com/culture/culture-news/ashley-flowers-nonprofit-dna-testing-cold-case-1197521/, accessed on 24 July 2022

McNeal, Stephanie (2019) The hosts of the popular podcast *Crime junkie* are accused of quietly deleting episodes over plagiarism, *BuzzFeed News*, 15 August. Available online at https://www.buzzfeednews.com/article/stephaniemcneal/crime-junkie-podcast-accused-plagiarism-episodes, accessed on 24 July 2022

Medium (2019) Breakaway podcast hit *Crime junkie* surpasses 18 million downloads in 2 months, 16 April. Available online at https://medium.com/cabana/breakaway-podcast-hit-crime-junkie-surpasses-18-million-downloads-in-two-months-88fe8c84303a, accessed on 22 March 2022

Penguin Random House (n.d.) *All good people here*. Available online at https://www.penguinrandomhouse.com/books/691141/all-good-people-here-by-ashley-flowers/, accessed on 22 March 2022

Punnett, Ian C. (2018) *Toward a theory of true crime narratives: A textual analysis*, Abingdon, Routledge

Quah, Nicholas (2019) A plagiarism scandal shakes up the true-crime podcast world, *Vulture*, 22 August. Available online at https://www.vulture.com/2019/08/crime-junkie-podcast-plagiarism-scandal.html, accessed on 24 July 2022

Rosman, Katherine (2022) Ashley Flowers wants to up the ante of true crime, 2 February. Available online at https://www.nytimes.com/2022/02/02/style/ashley-flowers-crime-junkie-deck.html, accessed on 24 July 2022

Saldaña, Johnny (2021 [2012]) *The coding manual for qualitative researchers*, London, Sage, fourth edition

Seale, Jack (2019) Are podcasts a disaster waiting to happen?, *Guardian*, 27 November. Available online at https://www.theguardian.com/tv-and-radio/2019/nov/27/why-podcasts-are-headed-for-disaster, accessed on 18 October 2022

Sharma, Megha (2020) This might be the reason why women are obsessed with true crime stories, *Vogue*, 20 February. Available online at https://www.vogue.in/culture-and-living/content/why-are-women-obsessed-with-true-crime-stories, accessed on 24 July 2022

Slakoff, Danielle C. (2021) The mediated portrayal of intimate partner violence in true crime podcasts: Strangulation, isolation, threats of violence, and coercive control, *Violence Against Women*, Available online at https://doi.org/10.1177/10778012211019055

SPJ code of ethics (2014) Society of Professional Journalists. Available online at https://www.spj.org/ethicscode.asp, accessed on 22 March 2022

Spangler, Todd (2019) *Crime junkie* podcast host Ashley Flowers responds to plagiarism allegations, *Variety*, 15 August. Available online at https://variety.com/2019/digital/news/crime-junkie-podcast-ashley-flowers-plagiarism-1203302072/?sub_action=logged_in, accessed on 24 July 2022

Smith, Sydney (2020) Top 5 plagiarism & attribution cases of 2019, *iMediaEthics*, 26 January. Available online at https://www.imediaethics.org/top-5-plagiarism-attribution-cases-of-2019/, accessed on 24 July 2022

Swan, Scott (2019) *Crime junkie* shares her passion in every podcast, *WTHR*, 25 March. Available online at https://www.wthr.com/article/news/trending-viral/crime-junkie-shares-her-passion-every-podcast/531-fc70fa37-68ed-4ce5-9a1a-3cc24272151d, accessed on 22 March 2022

Taylor, Derrick B. and Hauser, Christine (2019) Popular *Crime junkie* podcast removes episodes after plagiarism accusation, *The New York Times*, 22 August. Available online at https://www.nytimes.com/2019/08/22/business/media/crime-junkie-podcast-plagiarism.html, accessed on 24 July 2022

The Infinite Dial (2021) *Edison Research*, 11 March. Available online at https://www.edisonresearch.com/the-infinite-dial-2021-2/, accessed on 22 March 2022

Yardley, Elizabeth, Kelly, Emma and Robinson-Edwards, Shona (2019) Forever trapped in the imaginary of late capitalism? The serialized true crime podcast as a wake-up call in times of criminological slumber, *Crime Media Culture*, Vol. 15, No. 3 pp 503-521. Available online at https://doi.org/10.1177/1741659018799375

Wren, Adam (2019) The problem with *Crime junkie*, *Indianapolis Monthly*, 7 November. Available online at https://www.indianapolismonthly.com/longform/the-problem-with-crime-junkie, accessed on 22 March 2022

Note on the contributor

Kelli S. Boling is an Assistant Professor in the College of Journalism and Mass Communications at the University of Nebraska-Lincoln. Her research focuses on audience reception and representation in the media, especially genre-specific media and traditionally marginalised audiences based on gender or race.

Conflict of interest

There are no conflicts of interest or funding related to this research.

PAPER

Bethan Jones

Websleuthing, participatory culture and the ethics of true crime content

Interest in true crime has exploded throughout the last few years, with books, documentaries, TV shows and podcasts dominating the bestseller lists, ratings and airwaves. Yet changing digital technologies and changing audience/producer relationships have combined to encourage a form of participatory culture which brings with it its own ethical quandaries. From the erroneous naming of Brown University student Sunil Tripathi as the Boston Bomber on Reddit, to viral TikTok videos speculating over the disappearance and subsequent death of Gabby Petito, the line between investigation and entertainment is blurred. This paper examines participatory culture in the true crime community and questions the ethics of citizen investigation for real time cases on social media.

Keywords: participatory culture, true crime, ethics, Gabby Petito, social media

Introduction

Interest in true crime has exploded throughout the last few years, with books, documentaries, TV shows and podcasts dominating the bestseller lists, ratings and airwaves. Yet the genre has always attracted an audience. Jean Murley notes that true crime texts were hugely popular in the 1980s and 1990s, the books about 'real things that had happened to real people ... both terrifying and oddly reassuring' (2008: 1). In these books the killers are always caught and punished; no matter how evil the crime, justice prevails. With the rise of the internet, however, true crime audiences have access to a far wider range of cases and sources, not all of which are successfully closed. Between 2001 and 2003, for example, a serial killer was at work in Baton Rouge. Having killed five women and suspected of murdering more, rallies sponsored by families of the victims in association with a support group called Citizens Against the Serial Killer were held, putting pressure on the police to bring the perpetrator to justice (Weeber 2013). With the Task Force pulled together to investigate the murders failing, criminologist Maurice Godwin set up a Yahoo! group for people living in Baton Rouge to discuss the case. More than 250 people joined, with Godwin acting as moderator, 'teacher, disciplinarian, negotiator, promoter [and] timekeeper' (Weeber 2007: 30). Godwin refused to allow speculation in the group, but members were allowed to offer theories provided these were in line with the facts (ibid). A range of blogs also appeared, reporting on current crimes, historical cases, victim demographics and race (see Murley 2008: chapter five). As more social networking sites appeared and new formats such as podcasts entered the ring, the opportunities for audiences to engage more with true crime content have bloomed. As Tanya Horeck points out:

> ... what has become evident is the extent to which the true crime genre has come to epitomise participatory media culture and, in particular, an increasingly prevalent notion of the listener or viewer as a 'desktop detective' or an 'internet sleuth'. (2019: 6-7)

One recent example of this is the disappearance of Gabby Petito in 2021. Although her disappearance in and of itself is not unusual, what is distinctive is the amount of interest generated in the case online, and the use of social media platforms in enabling everyday citizens to participate in the search for Petito. This paper is interested in the ethics of contemporary true crime fandom as it intersects with participatory culture. I do not explore issues around polluting evidence, affecting witnesses' memories, alerting suspects so that they can destroy evidence or evade capture, and so on – all of which reduces the chance of a fair trial and ultimately justice being served. Rather, I am interested in the *ways* in which people are engaging with true crime, especially current cases. I argue that engagement with these cases is performed in the same way as audiences respond to reality TV true crime podcasts – in other words, as fans. Audiences' fascination with crime has a long history, Joy Wiltenburg (2004) noting the production of broadsheets and pamphlets in sixteenth-century Germany which marked out the 'basic contours' of the true crime genre. Citing the Lutheran minister Burkard Waldis' 1551 pamphlet *A true and most horrifying account of how a woman tyrannically murdered her four children and also killed herself, at Weidenhausen near Eshwege in Hesse,* she points out Waldis's use of literary techniques, including the way he builds suspense and pathos through the depiction of the pursuit and ultimate death of each child, along with the use of dialogue often from the victims, which magnify the emotional impact of the crime for the reader. Daniel E. Williams, tracing the history of crime literature in America, highlights the creation of a sympathetic view of the criminal and notes that the publication in 1784 of *The American Bloody Register*, America's first criminal magazine, led to the publication of full length 'rogue narratives', seeing the conclusion of 'a movement from fact to fiction, from the possibility of a story to a partial story, to a full story' (1983: 17). This storification of crime coincided with an increasing number of police forces as well as scientific advances in detection which, Pamela Burger suggests, 'shaped the public's interest in true crime mysteries' (Burger 2016). She examines the Lizzie Borden case, arguing that 'The sheer breadth of literature and art produced in its wake speaks to an enduring fascination with a story that was, in its day, nothing short of a media phenomenon' (ibid) with media outlets sharing daily updates and readers debating the minute details of the case and the criminal. This fascination is evident in other well-known crime cases. The murders of several prostitutes around the Whitechapel area of London in the 1880s gave rise to scores of lurid reports in the Victorian press, with L. Perry Curtis noting that 'the absence of any "reasonable" explanation for these mutilation murders stimulated all kinds of speculation by journalists and readers' (2001: 16). Indeed, newspapers published several letters from readers speculating on the identity of Jack the Ripper, his motives and ways through which he could be caught.

These two cases point not only to the fascination audiences have with accounts of criminality, but to the increasing role of audiences in investigating true crime. As technology progresses, so too do the ways in which audiences become involved. From writing letters to the editor to phoning in tips to *Crimewatch* to collating information on social media platforms and sharing details of suspected criminals, audience engagement with true crime has begun to blur the boundaries between police and public. Andrew Keen argues that the democratisation offered by Web 2.0 'is undermining truth, souring civic discourse, and belittling expertise, experience, and talent' (2011: 15), and while audiences can certainly aid the police and other law enforcement in their investigations, they also raise ethical implications which extend beyond the realms of fandom.

Contemporary true crime and participatory culture

Rachel Franks notes: 'The true crime genre has enjoyed significant stability in terms of popularity, though changes in format and focus have made the category an unstable one that has experienced several watershed moments' (2016: 240). One of those watershed moments occurred in the mid-2010s, when emerging technologies like podcasting converged with the participatory culture of the internet. The *Serial* podcast, from the creators of *This American life* and hosted by Sarah Koenig, debuted in October 2014 with season one revisiting the murder of high school student Hae Min Lee in 1999. Told across 12 episodes, Koenig focuses on Lee's boyfriend, Adnan Syed, who was found guilty of her murder yet maintains his innocence.[1] Although Koenig draws no conclusions, the podcast captured listeners' imaginations and broke records as the fastest podcast ever to reach 5 million downloads on Apple's iTunes store (Dredge 2014). *Serial* was followed in 2015 by two documentaries: HBO's *The jinx: The life and deaths of Robert Durst*, originally released in February; and Netflix's *Making a murderer*, season one of which was released in the December. *The jinx* runs for six episodes and deals with the unsolved disappearance of Durst's wife Kathy in 1982, the murder of writer Susan Berman in 2000 and the killing and dismemberment of Durst's neighbour in 2001. The documentary uses a range of footage and techniques including news footage and archival interviews, re-enactments, contemporary interviews and self-reflexive recordings by the documentary's writer/director Andrew Jarecki. Unlike *Serial* which comes to no conclusion about Syed's guilt or innocence, *The jinx* ends with Durst leaving an interview with Jarecki to go to the bathroom where, apparently unaware that his microphone was still recording, he made a rambling statement ending with an apparent confession. *Making a murderer*, a Netflix original series, aired its first season nine months after the final episode of *The jinx* but, similar to *Serial* its focus is on the potential framing of Steven Avery, convicted along with his nephew Brendan Dassey of the murder of Teresa Halbach in 2005. Season one spends its 10 episodes discussing Avery's 1985 conviction of murder, his subsequent exoneration and release, the civil suit he filed against Manitowoc County, his 2005 arrest and investigation, trial and conviction. It also examines the arrest, prosecution, and conviction of Dassey. The second season

Bethan Jones

examines the aftermath of both convictions on the respective families, the investigation undertaken by Kathleen Zellner, Avery's new attorney, which supports the thesis of Avery's innocence, and the efforts of Dassey's legal team to argue that his confession was coerced and his constitutional rights violated.

Each of these texts received wide acclaim and a large, international audience, but they also generated discussion – and in some cases action – online. When the first season of *Serial* concluded with no definitive answer for who killed Hae Min Lee fans created a forum on popular internet site Reddit to continue examining the murder (Berry 2015; Yardley et al. 2016, 2017). Set up in October 2014, with more than 70,000 members at the time of writing, the subreddit is 'a place for listeners to find information about the podcast and to discuss theories, predictions and other aspects of the show and case'. Participation is thus key to the community, and the season one wiki includes a collection of links to topics, maps, phone logs, timelines and evidence collated and updated by community members. Among the topics discussed on the subreddit is an analysis of *The Intercept*'s interview with Jay Wilds, one of the key witnesses in the case, which received more than 3,000 comments. These range from memes to speculation about Jay's motives to analysis of call logs refuting some of the claims he makes and while some are tongue in cheek (one redditor wrote '*rips notes, pictures, and diagrams off the wall. Well, its back to square one, you guys...'), they nevertheless highlight the active type of engagement and participation fans develop throughout the course of the podcast.

We see a similar pattern of behaviour in relation to *Making a murderer*, where fans created online resources to continue investigating after the first season finished. Gregory Stratton notes how Reddit users 'scoured for evidence from the documentary, statements in the media, and the trial, and explored the potentials for new evidence using the tools available to them' (2019: 188). The nature of Reddit means that members of the community are able to collate resources in one place and pool their shared knowledge to collaborate on the investigation, including the use of other websites. An interactive 'Remaking a murderer' map of the Avery property was created with important sites 'pinned' and a timeline of events as well as details of cell towers and key points during the investigation included. Another Reddit user posted satellite images of the Avery yard taken one month before and one month after Halbach's murder in case other users might be able to find something significant. While commenters point out some of the issues with the images – Google was not updated in that time period; the images were not hi-res; there was a lot of cloud cover – there were nevertheless further discussions both in that thread and the wider subreddit about how users could gather more data. Actions were also carried out offline, however, with two petitions requesting pardons for Avery and Dassey circulating in early 2016 resulting in the overturning of Dassey's conviction in the November, although it was reinstated the following year.

Less charitable acts were also carried out by viewers, however. Ken Kratz, prosecutor in the Avery case, began receiving death threats shortly after the series aired while Dassey's lawyer, Len Kachinsky, received hate mail for encouraging him to make a confession (Marsh 2016). Others left reviews on the Yelp page for Kratz's new law practice referring to both his conduct in the Avery case and his sexual harassment of a former client which led to his resignation in 2010 (Griffin 2015). Rodriquez argues: 'The digital era means that motivated viewers (and listeners) can conceptualise programs not as an end product, but a prompt for additional discussion' (2017: 133). Certainly, this is the case for *Serial*, *Making a murderer* and the scores of other true crime texts that have emerged throughout the past decade, but victims and families are also impacted by the participatory nature of the digital era.

Both Adnan Syed's older brother and Hae Min Lee's younger brother joined Reddit and began posting about the podcast on the *Serial* subreddit. Tanveer, Syed's brother, initially joined to correct misinformation quoted about himself (Dean 2014) but he also provided insights into his family's social context and attempted to cast doubt about his brother's guilt (Yardley et al. 2016). Yardley et al. point out that Tanveer wrote two posts on the subreddit but also joined discussions in 53 other threads, leaving 120 comments. On the contrary, Hae Min Lee's younger brother made fewer contributions – one post and five comments – and the tone of his content was far more scathing. In his post, titled I am Hae's brother – Do not AMA [Ask Me Anything], he criticised *Serial* fans for treating the case like fiction, writing:

> TO ME ITS [sic] REAL LIFE. To you listeners, its [sic] another murder mystery, crime drama, another episode of CSI. You weren't there to see your mom crying every night,

having a heartattck when she got the new [sic] that the body was found, and going to court almost everyday for a year seeing your mom weeping, crying and fainting. You don't know what we went through. Especially to those who are demanding our family response and having a meetup... you guys are disgusting.

Responses to his post were mainly positive, users expressing sympathy for the family's loss and arguing that – to many listeners – it is not simply a story but an event with which they empathise. Others responded more negatively, however, arguing that Koenig and the producers structure the series as a murder mystery which is why it fascinated so many (Widmerpoool70), pointing out that the podcast was not about Hae Min Lee but about Adnan Syed 'who is rotting in jail, and may be innocent' (paulogoulard); or arguing that those listening to the podcast 'aren't monsters, and we don't need to feel shame for taking an interest in what happened' (dogerwaul). As Yardley et al. note, Hae's brother 'appears to push back against his sister as public property, asserting ownership over her and his grief for her' (2016: 479) but the nature of the digital era means that the lines between private and public are blurred, leading some users to take on the role of internet detectives or 'websleuths', working alongside – or sometimes at odds with – law enforcement agencies.

Websleuthing and the ethics of true crime content

Websleuthing, according to Yardley et al. 'is the embodiment of participatory media, where the lines between the producer, consumer and subject are blurred, there are fewer restrictions in relation to time and space and online activities have real world, embodied consequences' (2018: 82). The emergence of Web 2.0 and the proliferation of websites like Wikipedia, YouTube and Twitter means that anyone can create, publish, share and comment on a range of texts without necessarily thinking about the real-world consequences of doing so. Perhaps one of the most infamous examples of this is the involvement of redditors in the search for the 2013 Boston Marathon bombing suspects. Shortly after the bombing a subreddit, r/findbostonbombers, was set up. Photographs taken by those at the marathon were posted to the forum in an effort to find those responsible. Three suspects were initially identified, Salaheddin Barhoum, Yassine Zaimi and Sunil Tripathi, with Barhoum and Zaimi appearing on the cover of the *New York Post* as persons of interest. Medieros (2019) points out that Barhoum and Zaimi were quickly ruled out as suspects by redditors, and indeed both sued the *New York Post* citing emotional harm from their identification in the paper. Some news outlets nevertheless pushed the idea that the 'witch hunt' against the men 'had been precipitated by social media "vigilantes"' (ibid: 9). Where Reddit could take some responsibility, however, was in the discussion surrounding Sunil Tripathi. Tripathi disappeared a month before the bombings and this, coupled with a tweet from a former classmate, resulted in posts identifying Tripathi as the bomber posted to the subreddit. Although these were eventually locked, redditors convinced of his guilt took the rumours elsewhere: 'People then began posting on the family's Facebook page [set up to help find him] that he was behind the bombings' (Thirtydegress 2013 quoted in Medieros 2019); his family received scores of emails and the organisations that had helped in the search for Tripathi turned their backs for fear of aiding a 'terrorist' (Kang 2013). Tripathi's body was eventually recovered on 23 April 2013; he had committed suicide before the bombing happened.

There are clearly ethical issues in the way each of these wrongful identifications was handled. The former raise questions about quality standards in traditional media: who was fact-checking claims before publishing them?; what language was being used when identifying people of interested in an ongoing investigation? The latter, however, raises questions about the role of social media and the responsibility of users to consider what, and how, they are posting online. Almost a decade later these questions remain, compounded by the growth in social media platforms, the renewed interest in true crime and the integration of participatory culture into the mainstream. The disappearance of Gabby Petito is perhaps one of the best examples of the convergence between true crime and participatory culture, and the ethical implications of this shifting media landscape.

Petito began a US-wide road trip with her fiancé Brian Laundrie in July 2021. Posts were made regularly on her Instagram and the TikTok account they shared until late August 2021 but it was not until two days after her mother reported her missing, on 11 September, that the case began to make waves on social media. Comedian Paris Campbell posted a video about the case on TikTok on 13 September, sharing a missing person's poster she saw in an article but also raising questions about her disappearance (2021). Campbell highlighted

Bethan Jones

that Petito went on a road trip with Laundrie and went missing before Laundrie returned home alone. She shared pictures of Laundrie's Instagram, highlighting the point at which the photographs moved from being of the pair of them to of Laundrie alone, indicating that Petito's mother received a text but was not able to verify if it was from her daughter, and stated that 'this whole thing seems really bad'. Haley Toumaian, another TikToker, was drawn to the case because she 'saw a lot of myself in what was being reported about her' (Lucas 2021) and also shared theories on her channel. One of the videos she posted included an in-depth analysis of the last photo on Petito's Instagram account (2021). In it she argues that the photo, captioned with 'Happy Halloween' and two emojis, was not in keeping with Petito's usual style, which was more in depth, detailing her travels and tagging the location.

Campbell and Toumaian are two of the most prominent TikTokers posting about Petito, and are the two most often identified, and interviewed, in news articles about the case (Gault 2021; Lucas 2021; Rosman 2021). The videos they post often contain unverified information, including updates on the discovery of a body thought to be Laundrie's and an apparent photo of Petito in the background of a photo on Reddit. Toumaian does post updates when information she provides is found out to be false and Campbell also shared videos debunking myths and misinformation on the case, but both are also involved in 'investigating data that had not yet been acquired by official investigators, getting information from authorities, attempting to reach out to the family, and reposting it' (Aguilar et al. 2021).

These websleuthing practices are echoed across a range of social media platforms. By Friday 17 September, less than a week after Petito went missing, the tag #gabbypetito had received over 77 million views on TikTok, with #findgabbypetito receiving 16.6 million and #gabbypetitoupdate 7.3 million. The r/GabbyPetito subreddit was created on 13 September, and had 33,200 members in its first four days and Petito was also the subject of multiple threads in the r/True Crime and r/TrueCrimeDiscussion subreddits. This behaviour reflects what we have already seen with other true crime podcasts and documentaries, but the main difference between the Petito case and that of, say, *Making a murderer* is that these activities were taking place in real time. Rather than a documentary or podcasts aired after the fact, where those involved have had time to come to terms with the events and to begin to manage their grief, the Petito case was treated like a developing narrative. The storyline evolved with each new update – whether that came from news sources or from social media users themselves. And these websleuths used a variety of additional digital tools including geotags from the couple's Instagram posts, information from AllTrails, their Spotify listening habits and Pinterest account activity to draw up a timeline of events and speculate as to what happened (Aguilar et al. 2021). The release of body cam footage from police responding to a 911 call on 12 August resulted in analyses of the footage for clues as to Petito's state of mind as well as discussions about domestic abuse, gaslighting and coercive control (Beeman 2021; Devine 2021; Crime Analyst 2021).

Jessica Goldstein, writing about the ethics of *Serial*, says: 'By employing a multitude of tactics typically utilised in fiction – cliffhangers, hunches, personal asides – Koenig's narration lands somewhere between straight reporting and something more personal' (2014). These elements are evident in TikToks and subreddits, which not only secure the audience's attention but encourage it to join the narrative dots. Indeed, one podcast – *Crime junkie* – released a special episode on the Gabby Petito 'breaking story'. Host Ashley Flowers states: 'In almost four years of doing this show I have never, I mean never, seen you guys in a frenzy like you are in now. Our emails are flooded. Our DMs are flooded. It is the only thing you want to talk about in the fan club' (2021). The Monday following the airing, the episode was the fifth most popular on Spotify's podcast charts and No. 1 on Apple Podcasts (Rosman 2021).

There is an argument here that some began sharing content about Petito in order to further their own agenda – an argument levelled against reality TV star, Dog the Bounty Hunter, and former host of *America's most wanted*, John Walsh (Graziosi 2021). People do, of course, capitalise on true crime. The documentaries and podcasts discussed in this paper generate profits for their producers and highlight the profiles of lawyers and journalists whose careers may skyrocket as a result. What is more unethical in the case of Petito, however, is the fact that this speculation comes in real time, and that those doing so are not subject to the same ethical or technical boundaries that journalists and filmmakers are. Abbie Richards points out: 'There's a lot of people who are capitalizing off of and profiting off of creating content that's designed to dissect the last days that we know of this girl' (in Anders and Kornfield 2021). That this is done at the same time as the investigation, rather than at a remove when the family has time to grieve, feels particularly immoral, as Richards argues in a Twitter thread: 'The way true crime turns real people's trauma into entertainment for profit is already disgusting. But watching it unfold in real time with Gabby Petito's case is nauseating' (2021). While some TikTokers argue that they were posting information in order to spread awareness about Petito's disappearance, the amount of time spent examining her social media activities, analysing minute details and sharing them online blurs the boundaries between investigation and voyeurism.

Here I refer to the mediated voyeurism Clay Calvert describes as 'the consumption of revealing images of and information about others' apparently real and unguarded lives, often yet not always for purposes of entertainment but frequently at the expense of privacy and disclosure, through the mass media and internet' (2004: 2). The concept of voyeurism is often tied to notions of sexual deviance, which is not applicable to what I discuss in this paper. However, Calvert argues it is important to keep this definition in mind as it suggests there are forms of watching or looking that are inappropriate and 'fall outside the boundary of acceptable conduct' (2004: 52). I argue that speculation about Petito was voyeuristic in a way that speculation about past cases is less so. *Serial* and *Making a murderer*, for example, detail events that happened years ago. The alleged perpetrators are jailed and justice served.

The narratives around the cases thus emphasise justice for the wrongfully convicted and encourage a form of citizen investigation in order to right that wrong. In the Petito case no such narrative was in place: at the beginning it was a missing person's case, and only after the poring over of video content did social media users begin to suspect foul play. What also takes this real-time speculation over an ethical boundary is the lack of critical distance displayed by those posting on social media. Jessica Dean, whose younger brother was friends with the girls convicted in the 2014 Slender Man stabbing and so witnessed the effect that interest in the case had on those involved, criticises the obsession with the Petito case in a now deleted TikTok video captioned 'Tone deaf true crime Tiktok right now'. She parodies those posting about the case:

> Oh, you haven't heard of Gabby Petito? Oh my god, girl, you are missing out. This stuff is so good. I made a 28-part monetised series on my TikTok all about it, going over every single detail, including her Spotify playlist. I just dig up every inch of this poor girl's life for my personal entertainment' (in Chen 2021).

Although we can argue that there were more altruistic motives, there was nevertheless some excitement about being involved in the search – whether that resulted in Petito being found alive or 'solving' the case before the FBI did. Many of the videos shared on TikTok and comments posted in response to them express an element of glee about being involved – even tangentially – with the investigation. Yet as one respondent to Richards' tweet sardonically replies: '"We're witnessing a true crime documentary happening in real time!!!11!" actually, megan, a true crime documentary happening in real time is just called a tragedy' (1randomdude4 2021). This inability, or lack of desire, to separate the evolving case from the actual tragedy leads to one of the most challenging ethical considerations in the convergence between true crime and participatory culture. When documentaries and podcasts demand the audience's involvement, at times encouraging engagement across a range of platforms, it becomes a normal way of engaging with any text: responses like 'I never thought TikTok would have me to into something so deep' and 'I swear tiktok is going to solve this case before the FBI let's goooo fam!' only reiterate the blurring of lines.

Conclusion

I noted in the introduction to this paper that true crime is a genre that always attracted audiences. Yet, as I outline, the convergence of true crime, digital platforms and participatory culture opened the door for what we might think of as citizen investigation, or websleuthing, and the ethical questions that come with it. Cox et al. note: 'As a genre, true crime is part documentary, part mystery, and part invitation' (2019: 40) and the invitation is extended even further thanks to the growth of social media platforms. The way in which the TikTok algorithm works, in particular, ensures that scores of these videos are pushed into users' 'for you' pages regardless of whether the person posting the video is involved in the case, is providing accurate information or is simply furthering a conspiracy theory (Aguilar et al. 2021). The blurring of the lines between participation and investigation, fact and fiction raises questions about the ethics of creating and consuming true crime not previously considered.

Of course, law enforcement has long appealed to audiences to provide tips, evidence or theories about crimes. The sourcing of information from the public is nothing new, and the move to crowdsourcing information and citizen investigation given technological changes comes as no surprise. Nhan et al. argue:

> … there is clearly a need for public officials to create regulatory and other strategies by which they can direct public involvement in ways that reduce the potential for harm – such as that occurs through the misidentification of individuals as 'suspects' – while maximizing opportunities for generating useful tips, having communities serve as 'eyes and ears' and other activities of investigational and other use to law enforcement. (2017: 342)

There is also an increasing need for law enforcement and social media platforms to work together to prevent these harms. In the case of the Boston bombing, it is likely that the FBI asked Reddit to have certain threads removed and to ensure tighter moderation of threads (Nhan et al. 2017). Redditors were also encouraged to contact the police or the FBI with any information that might be pertinent to the case. Although the videos posted to TikTok did result in scores of phone calls to the police, an overwhelming number of users posted speculation with the hope of being the 'first' to propose a useful theory or to crack the case and receive accolades for doing so. As much as users interested in true crime might consider themselves a community, when it comes to attempts to solve cases like Gabby Petito's, there is a need for a communal approach to the ethics of these investigations within participatory culture: what tactics are being used and what harms might they engender for both the victim and the family?; who is profiting from the content produced?; how and why?; and are the cultural practices of fandom appropriate for this kind of citizen investigation?

Note

[1] Syed's conviction was quashed in September 2022 after prosecutors said a year-long review of the case had found two alternative suspects. On 11 October 2022 Syed was cleared of the charges, new DNA tests showing that he was not involved in Lee's death and had been wrongfully convicted

References

1randomdude4 (2021) 'We're witnessing a true crime documentary happening in real time!!!11!' actually, megan, a true crime documentary happening in real time is just called a tragedy, *Twitter*. Available online at https://twitter.com/1randomdude4/status/1439671726456164363, accessed on 18 August 2022

Aguilar, Gabrielle, Ompolasvili, Sofia, Garcia Amaya, Luisa and Kerstens, Sophie (2021) True crime TikTok: Affording criminal investigation and media visibility in the Gabby Petito case, *Masters of Media*. Available online at https://mastersofmedia.hum.uva.nl/blog/2021/10/29/true-crime-tiktok-affording-criminal-investigation-and-media-visibility-in-the-gabby-petito-case/, accessed on 6 April 2022

Anders, Caroline and Kornfield, Meryl (2021) A throng of internet sleuths are on the Gabby Petito case. Why has it sparked so much interest? *Washington Post*, 21 September. Available online at https://www.washingtonpost.com/nation/2021/09/18/gabby-petito-case-tiktok-sleuths/, accessed on 6 April 2022

Beeman, Amy (2021) Body language expert breaks down the police video of Gabby Petito, *Grunge*, 23 September. Available online at https://www.grunge.com/611697/body-language-expert-breaks-down-the-police-video-of-gabby-petito/, accessed on 6 April 2022

Berry, Richard (2015) A golden age of podcasting? Evaluating *Serial* in the context of podcast histories, *Journal of Radio & Audio Media*, Vol. 22, No. 2 pp 170-178

Burger, Pamela (2016) The bloody history of the true crime genre, *JSTOR Daily*, 24 August. Available at https://daily.jstor.org/bloody-history-of-true-crime-genre, accessed on 6 April 2022

Campbell, Paris (2021) Gabby Petito. *@stopitparis*. Available online at https://www.tiktok.com/@stopitparis/video/7007529819135053062. accessed on 6 April 2022

Chen, Tanya (2021) TikTok's obsession with the Gabby Petito case is sparking a debate over how much true crime fans are really helping, *Buzzfeed News*, 20 September. Available online at https://www.buzzfeednews.com/article/tanyachen/tiktoks-obsession-with-the-gabby-petito-case, accessed on 6 April 2022

Cox, Courtney, Ralston, Devon and Wood, Charles (2019) Negotiating ethics of participatory investigation in true crime podcasts, *Proceedings of the Computers & Writing Conference*. Available at https://wac.colostate.edu/docs/proceedings/cw2019/chapter3.pdf, accessed on 6 April 2022

Crime Analyst (2021) Episode 80: 'The murder of Gabby Petito, Part 5', *Audioboom*. Available online at https://audioboom.com/posts/8105917-the-crime-analyst-ep-80-the-murder-of-gabby-petito-part-5, accessed on 18 August 2022

Crime junkie (2021) MISSING: Gabby Petito, *Apple Podcasts*. Available online at https://podcasts.apple.com/us/podcast/missing-gabby-petito/id1322200189?i=1000546245453, accessed on 1 September 2022

Dean, Michelle (2014) Serial nears its end, but the Reddit detectives keep working, *Guardian*, 11 December. Available online at http://www.theguardian.com/tv-and-radio/2014/dec/11/serial-nears-end-reddit-detectives-keep-working, accessed on 6 April 2022

Devine, Lucy (2021) Gabby Petito followers spot Youtuber's 'hidden hand signals for help' in Bodycam footage, *Tyla*. Available online at https://www.tyla.com/life/gabby-petito-death-body-cam-footage-brian-laundrie-hand-signal-moab-20211018, accessed on 6 April 2022

Dredge, Stuart (2014) Serial podcast breaks iTunes records as it passes 5m downloads and streams, *Guardian*, 18 November. Available online at https://www.theguardian.com/technology/2014/nov/18/serial-podcast-itunes-apple-downloads-streams, accessed on 16 April 2022

Franks, Rachel (2016) True crime: The regular reinvention of a genre, *Journal of Asia-Pacific Pop Culture*, Vol. 1, No. 2 pp 239-254

Gault, Matthew (2021) Inside TikTok's amateur investigation into Gabby Petito's disappearance, *Vice*, 20 September. Available online at https://www.vice.com/en/article/pkb5j8/gabby-petito-internet-sleuth-investigation-tiktok-instagram-spotify, accessed on 6 April 2022

Goldstein, Jessica (2014) The complicated ethics of *Serial*, the most popular podcast of all time, *Think Progress*, 21 November. Available online at https://archive.thinkprogress.org/the-complicated-ethics-of-serial-the-most-popular-podcast-of-all-time-6f84043de9a9/, accessed on 6 April 2022

Grazioso, Graig (2021) Laundrie attorney slams Dog the Bounty Hunter, John Walsh for using Gabby Petito case to feed their 'egos', *Independent*, 14 October. Available online at https://www.independent.co.uk/news/world/americas/crime/dog-the-bounty-hunter-john-walsh-gabby-petito-b1938634.html, accessed on 30 August 2022

Griffin, Tamerra (2015) People are writing scathing Yelp reviews for the prosecutor from 'Making a murderer', *Buzzfeed*, 26 December. Available online at https://www.buzzfeednews.com/article/tamerragriffin/people-are-writing-scathing-yelp-reviews-for-the-prosecutor, accessed on 6 April 2022

Horeck, Tanya (2019) *Justice on demand true crime in the digital streaming era*, Detroit, Wayne State University Press

Kang, Jay Caspian (2013) Should Reddit be blamed for the spreading of a smear? *New York Times Magazine*, 25 July. Available online at http://www.nytimes.com/2013/07/28/magazine/should-reddit-be-blamed-for-the-spreading-of-a-smear.html accessed on 26 April 2022

Lucas, Jessica (2021) Meet the TikTokers fixated on the Gabby Petito case, *Input*. Available online at https://www.inputmag.com/culture/tiktok-gabby-petito-case-social-media, accessed on 6 April 2022

Marsh, Laura (2016) Murder, they wrote, *Dissent*, Vol. 63, No. 2 pp 6-11

Medeiros, Ben (2019) User-generated content and the regulation of reputational harm: The Boston Marathon bombing as case study, *Communication Law Review*, Vol. 19, No. 1 pp 1-28

Murley, Jean (2008) *The rise of true crime: 20thcentury murder and American popular culture*, Connecticut, Praeger

Nhan Johnny, Huey, Laura and Broll, Ryan (2015) Digilantism: An analysis of crowdsourcing and the Boston Marathon bombings, *British Journal of Criminology*, Vol. 57 pp 341-361

Perry Curtis Jr., L. (2001) *Jack the Ripper & the London press*, New Haven, Connecticut, Yale University Press

Richards, Abbie (@abbieasr) (2021) The way true crime turns real people's trauma into entertainment for profit is already disgusting. But watching it unfold in real time with Gabby Petito's case is nauseating. So let's explore TikTok users' unhealthy obsession with her disappearance. *Twitter*. Available online at https://twitter.com/abbieasr/status/1438580799603892232, accessed on 6 April 2022

Rodriquez, Nathan J. (2017) Digital pitchforks: Justice-gone-wrong narratives in popular culture, Madere, Carol M. (ed.) *Viewpoints on media effects: Pseudo-reality and its influence on media consumers*, Idaho Falls, Idaho, Lexington Books pp 133-148

Rosman, Katherine (2021) How the case of Gabrielle Petito galvanized the internet, *New York Times*. Available online at https://www.nytimes.com/2021/09/20/style/gabby-petito-case-tiktok-social-media.html, accessed on 6 April 2022

Stratton, Gregory (2019) Wrongful conviction, pop culture, and achieving justice in the digital age, Dimitris, Akrivos and Antoniou, Alexandros K. (eds) *Crime, deviance and popular culture*, London, Palgrave Macmillan pp 177-201

Toumaian, Haley (2021) Reply to @laurenlee, *robandhaley* Available online at https://www.tiktok.com/@robandhaley/video/7008941768121011462, accessed on 6 April 2022

Weeber, Stan (2007) *In search of Derrick Todd Lee: The internet social movement that made a difference*, Lanham, MD, University Press of America

Weeber, Stan C. (2013) Online citizens, missing persons and the police: Three case studies, *Southeastern Social Science Journal*, Vol. 2 pp 5-15

Williams, Daniel. E. (1983) Rogues, rascals and scoundrels: The underworld literature of Early America, *American Studies*, Vol. 24, No. 2 pp 5-19

Wiltenburg, Joy (2004) True crime: The origins of modern sensationalism, *The American Historical Review*, Vol. 109, No. 5 pp 1377-1404

Yardley, Elizabeth, Lynes, Adam George Thomas, Wilson, David and Kelly, Emma (2016) What's the deal with 'websleuthing'? News media representations of amateur detectives in networked spaces, *Crime, Media, Culture*, Vol. 1 pp 1-29

Yardley, Elizabeth, Wilson, David and Kennedy, Morag (2017) 'TO ME ITS [SIC] REAL LIFE': Secondary victims of homicide in newer media, *Victims & Offenders*, Vol. 12, No. 3 pp 467-496

Note on the contributor

Bethan Jones is a Research Associate at the University of York. She writtes extensively about anti-fandom, media tourism and participatory cultures, and is co-editor of *Crowdfunding the future: Media industries, ethics and digital society* (Peter Lang) and the forthcoming *Participatory culture wars: Controversy, conflict, and complicity in fandom* (under contract with University of Iowa Press). Bethan is on the board of the Fan Studies Network, co-chair of the SCMS Fan and Audience Studies Scholarly Interest Group and one of the incoming editorial team for the journal *Popular Communication*.

Conflict of interest

The author received no funding for this research or publication.

ARTICLE

Nina Jones

Curing an ethical hangover: A forensic examination of the potential of the post-true crime movement

The boom in contemporary true crime documentary is beginning to subside, leaving in its wake a complex ethical hangover. A 'post-true crime' movement has responded with an attempt to redress and reframe the genre by resituating victims' stories within the narrative, and increasing the representation of stories from LGBT+ communities and non-white perspectives.

But what subjective and emotional values are proposed by the genre that separates it from its predecessors? And, if these films or series share similar motifs and tropes, how are they supporting the post-true crime movement? This video essay touches upon the origins of the term 'post-true crime' and develops it further through utilising a variety of audio-visual texts, including the particularly controversial example of HBO's The jinx (2015) and the seemingly progressive series HBO's I'll be gone in the dark (2020). Through this, the video essay begins to unpack these complex questions and proposes that an ethical code for true crime could be a reality.

Link to video essay

https://vimeo.com/742671641

References

Visual and audio sources

48 Hours (2015) *Robert Durst lawyer speaks out about secretly recorded audio and his client's arrest*. Available online at https://www.youtube.com/watch?v=ayYBp5yiOEk, accessed on 4 June 2022

ABC News (2015) *The jinx*: Robert Durst arrested, new information discovered, 17 March. Available online at https://www.youtube.com/watch?v=IgmXzTzfKiY&t=8s, accessed on 4 June 2022

ABC News (2015) Robert Durst's alleged trail of crimes, 21 March. Available online at https://www.youtube.com/watch?v=TmoB20h0TF8&t=137s, accessed on 4 June 2022

ABC News Australia (2017) The questionable ethics of the true crime podcast, 4 November. Available online at https://www.youtube.com/watch?v=ap4Oxb88MRw&t=199s, accessed on 16 June 2022

Berlinger, Joe and Sinofsky, Bruce (1992) *My brother's keeper*, USA, Creative Thinking International Ltd

Berlinger, Joe (2019) *Conversations with a killer: The Ted Bundy tapes*, USA, Netflix

Campos, Antonio (2022) *The staircase mini series*, USA, Warner Bros. Discovery Global Streaming & Interactive Entertainment

Cheddar Now (2019) *The jinx* filmmakers allegedly manipulated Robert Durst's confession, 1 May. Available online at https://www.youtube.com/watch?v=4P7opPozKZM&t=141s, accessed on 12 June 2022

De Lestrade, Jean Xavier (2004) *The staircase*, France, Canal + (Episodes 1-10) Netflix (Episodes 11-13)

E! Insider (2022) Why Toni Collette thinks *The staircase* is 'so honest', *E! Red Carpet & Award Shows*. Available online at https://www.youtube.com/watch?v=6PA4AQHi_H4&t=42s, accessed on 11 June 2022

Garbus, Liz (2020) *I'll be gone in the dark*, USA, HBO Documentary Film

Goode, Eric and Chaiklin, Rebecca (2020) *Tiger king*, USA, Netflix

Jarecki, Andrew (2015) *The jinx*, USA, HBO Documentary Films

Langley, John and Babour, Malcolm (1989) *Cops*, USA, Fox

London Live (2018) Jean-Xavier de Lestrade & Matthieu Belghiti discuss truth & *The staircase*, London Live. Available online at https://www.youtube.com/watch?v=Mxpzza702CE&t=1s, accessed on 9 June 2022

Mather, John (1984) *Crime watch*, UK, BBC

Morris, Errol (1988) *The thin blue line*, USA, Miramax Films

Nantoli, Ryan and Hoepfner, Fran (2018) *The Onion podcasts: A very fateful murder*. Available online at https://podcasts.apple.com/us/podcast/episode-1-a-perfect-murder/id1333714430?i=1000401483940

Perrault, Dan and Yacenda, Tony (2017) *American vandal*, USA, Netflix

Popplewell, Jenny (2020) *American murder: The family nextdoor*, USA, Netflix

Russell, Tiller and Carroll, James (2021) *The night stalker: The hunt for a serial killer*, USA, Netflix

SNL (2021) *Murder show*. Available online at https://www.youtube.com/watch?v=J4RdcE6H4Gs&t=32s, accessed on 16 June 2022

Stanley Gardner, Erle and Steeger, Harry (1957) *The court of last resort*, USA, NBC

Turney, Sarah and Lordan, John (2021) Voices for Justices: Live at CrimeCon 2021: Ethics in true crime panel. Available online at https://podcasts.apple.com/gb/podcast/live-at-crimecon-2021-ethics-in-true-crime/id1469338483?i=1000526703473

Vile, Jesse and Wood, Ellena (2020) *The ripper*, UK, Netflix

Williams, Liza (2019) *The Yorkshire Ripper files: A very British crime story*, UK, BBC

Zeman, Joshua (2021) *The sons of Sam: A descent into darkness*, USA, Netflix

Text sources

Associated Press (2018) Oxygen media defends Natalee Holloway series amid mother's lawsuit, *Hollywood Reporter*, 7 February. Available online at https://www.hollywoodreporter.com/tv/tv-news/oxygen-media-defends-natalee-holloway-series-mothers-lawsuit-1082799/, accessed on 12 June 2022

Bolin, Alice (2018) The ethical dilemma of high brow true crime, *Vulture*, 1 August. Available online at https://www.vulture.com/2018/08/true-crime-ethics.html, accessed on 12 June 2022

Chan, Melissa (2020) Real people getting re-traumatised: The human cost of binge watching true crime series, *Time*, 24 April. Available online at https://time.com/5825475/true-crime-victim-families/, accessed on 12 June 2022

Dietz, Meredith (2021) Can you ethically enjoy true crime?, *Lifehacker*, 30 September. Available online at https://lifehacker.com/there-are-ways-to-consume-true-crime-more-ethically-1847770893, accessed on 14 June 2022

Elliott, Warren (2022) Why *The staircase* subject Michel Peterson is furious over HBO's series. Available online at https://screenrant.com/staircase-show-michael-peterson-criticism-response-angry/, accessed on 12 June 2022

Eloise, Marianna (2020) *I'll be gone in the dark*: The show bringing sensitivity to true crime TV, *Guardian*, 28 August. Available online at https://www.theguardian.com/tv-and-radio/2020/aug/28/ill-be-gone-in-the-dark-sensitivity-true-crime-tv-hbo, accessed on 14 June 2022

Fashingbauer Cooper, Gael (2018) *The Onion's* true-crime parody podcast delivers killer laughs, *CNET*, 5 February. Available online at https://www.cnet.com/culture/the-onion-a-very-fatal-murder-podcast-true-crime-parody/, accessed on 12 June 2022

Greene, Steve (2015) 'A very fateful murder': Even the fake ad's are hilarious in the *Onion*'s true crime podcast parady. Available online at https://www.yahoo.com/entertainment/very-fatal-murder-even-fake-200922631.html, accessed on 14 June 2022

Green, Elon (2020) The enduring, pernicious whiteness of true crime. Available online at https://theappeal.org/whiteness-of-true-crime/, accessed on 14 June 2022

Hook, Melissa (2004) The real CSI: Are crime victims being re-victimized by filmmakers? Available online at https://www.documentary.org/feature/real-csi-are-crime-victims-being-re-victimized-filmmakers, accessed on 12 June 2022

Jeffries, Stuart (2018) True crime 02: Is the genre running out of material or evolving?, *Guardian*, 25 October. Available online at https://www.theguardian.com/culture/2018/oct/25/true-20-is-the-genre-running-out-of-material-or-evolving, accessed on 12 June 2022

Joho, Jess (2021) Meet the true crime podcaster making your guilty pleasure more ethical, *Mashable*, 16 October. Available online at https://mashable.com/article/truer-crime-podcast-ethics-socal-justice, accessed on 14 June 2022

Keegan, Rebecca (2019) Inside 'Making a murderer' lawsuit and the hidden dangers of TV's true crime craze, *Hollywood Reporter*, 17 January. Available online at https://www.hollywoodreporter.com/movies/movie-features/inside-a-making-a-murderer-lawsuit-hidden-dangers-true-crime-tv-1176395/, accessed on 12 June 2022

Leszkiewicz, Anna (2021) From *Serial* to *Making a murderer*: Can true crime as entertainment ever be ethical? *New Statesman*, 15 January. Available online at https://www.newstatesman.com/culture/tv-radio/2016/01/serial-making-murderer-can-true-crime-entertainment-ever-be-ethical, accessed on 14 June 2022

Miller, Julie (2022) *The staircase* filmmakers feel 'betrayed' by HBO MAX's adaptation, *Vanity Fair*, 13 May. Available online at https://www.vanityfair.com/hollywood/2022/05/the-staircase-documentary-hbo-max, accessed on 12 June 2022

Miller, Laura (2020) Finally, a sensitive, intelligent true crime documentary series, *Slate*, 30 June. Available online at https://slate.com/culture/2020/06/michelle-mcnamara-hbo-documentary-review-golden-state-killer.html, accessed on 14 June 2022

Milian, Aidan (2021) The racial bias of true crime: Why is murder marketed to white women? Available online at https://metro.co.uk/2021/01/01/the-racial-bias-of-true-crime-why-is-murder-marketed-to-white-women-13615372/, accessed on 14 June 2022

Nussbaum, Emily (2015) The strange allure of Robert Durst and *The jinx*, *New Yorker*, 23 March. Available online at https://www.newyorker.com/magazine/2015/03/23/what-about-bob, accessed on 12 June 2022

Patten, Dominic (2016) Obama confirms he can't pardon *'Making a murderer'* Steven Avery. Available online at https://deadline.com/2016/01/making-a-murderer-no-obama-pardon-for-steven-avery-netflix-1201678213/, accessed on 12 June 2022

Paul, Anna (2022) How our true crime obsession created an army of armchair detectives, *Metro*, 9 April. Available online at https://metro.co.uk/2022/04/09/in-focus-how-our-true-crime-obsession-created-armchair-detectives-16416461/, accessed on 12 June 2022

Punnett, Ian Case (2018) *Toward a theory of true crime narratives*, New York, Routledge

Tait, Amelia (2021) The rise of 'citizen sleuths': The true crime buffs trying to solve true crime, *Guardian*, 2 October. Available online at https://www.theguardian.com/tv-and-radio/2021/oct/02/the-rise-of-citizen-sleuths-the-true-buffs-trying-to-solve-cases, accessed on 12 June 2022

Turney, Sarah (2022a) What happens when families & survivors start to fight back against unethical true crime content creators?, Twitter, 4 June. Available online at https://twitter.com/SarahETurney/status/1533166654779076608, accessed on 16 June 2022

Turney, Sarah (2022b) Hot take! We are people not cash cows, Twitter, 4 April. Available online at https://twitter.com/SarahETurney/status/1516467836125802506, accessed on 16 June 2022

Verdier, Hannah (2018) Could *A very fatal murder* kill off the true-crime podcast?, *Guardian*, 20 February. Available online at https://www.theguardian.com/tv-and-radio/2018/feb/20/could-a-very-fatal-kill-off-the-true-crime-podcast, accessed on 16 June 2022

Note on the contributors

Nina Jones is a practice-led PhD candidate at the University of Birmingham within the Department of Film and Creative Writing. Her research area of expertise is in contemporary true crime documentary ethics and the post-true crime genre. She uses audio visual experiments to analyse complex ethical dilemmas within the production and consumption of true crime documentaries. Her background is in professional documentary film editing and she is also a film tutor for undergraduate and postgraduate students. Her forthcoming documentary thesis is a reflection upon the complex nature of true crime documentary production and will challenge the role of the self when making conflicting ethical choices around narrative, aesthetics and representation.

Conflict of interest

No funding was received for the research presented in the paper.

BOOK REVIEWS

The BBC: A people's history
David Hendy
Profile Books, 2022 pp 570
ISBN: 9781781255254; ebk 9781782831945

This is a stunner of a book. Brilliantly researched and a great read. All 570 pages. It was even bigger but publisher sense prevailed and it is down to just a door-stopper. Hendy deserves plenty kudos for it.

He calls it *A people's history* and, unlike some other official BBC histories, it does reach down from the BBC brahmin caste to the depths of producers and cleaners at the corporation and the unseen – namely the audience. Hendy uses not just the comprehensive BBC Written Archives Centre but also the Mass Observation Archives at his Sussex University as his material for sources. In addition, he has interviewed some of the actors to the century-old drama that is the national broadcaster's eternal fate. 'This place is always in crisis,' as the current director general, Tim Davie, once told me.

The century starts in 1922 with the creation of the British Broadcasting Company. The corporation came five years later so maybe the BBC is celebrating prematurely this year! John Reith and his original lieutenants may have been visionary but in a very Presbyterian way: broadcasting to them was social medicine to be taken by the populace. Hence the JR triptych mission statement: 'Inform, educate and entertain.' The last was kept under Auntie's skirts until wartime on radio and on television until the launch of a competitor, ITV, in the mid-1950s.

Reith was a believer in command and control. That only really eased when Hugh Carleton Greene was appointed DG in 1960. He allowed in fresh air to the corporation yet relics of the original civil service structure are still there in today's BBC in the layers of bureaucracy. My first boss in the BBC, John Dekker, called them 'The Oxford Circus Thought Police'!

Hendy gets well into the warp and weft of the 'BBC Boss Class' as we rebels in Lime Grove (almost everybody) called them but also into the warp and weft of the BBC in British national life.

Sometimes it gets the national mood right, sometimes wrong. On the 1926 General Strike, Reith proclaimed the BBC was for the government and Winston Churchill. He was wrong. The corporation redeemed itself in spades since in the Second World War and more recently as the 'go to' source of trusted information during the covid pandemic and the current war in Ukraine. The BBC has simply got better at understanding and not talking at its audience over the decades. It has had to.

One audience it will never satisfy is the British political class: Nadine Dorries, surely the worst culture secretary in a very crowded field, and her 'whack-a-mole' tactics on the licence fee just the latest iteration. Politicians, of all shades, seem unable to distinguish a public from a state broadcaster. It belongs to the licence payers – not the party in power. Boris Johnson, like his role model Winston Churchill, thought that by huffing and puffing they will blow the BBC house down. They won't so long as the BBC retains the public's trust.

Stacking the board of governors (whatever it is currently called) and a friendly DG are commonplace. New Labour did it with Gavyn Davies and Greg Dyke; the current government are doing it with the chair, Richard Sharp, who is an open Tory, and Tim Davie the current DG, who is a recovering Tory. That ideology, though, does not give them a free pass to the levers of power as the current freezing of the licence fee shows.

Hendy chronicles well the attempts over the century to 'tame' the BBC. Sometimes directly with their man/woman on the inside, sometimes not. Usually it fails, but like a wounded wild beast the corporation becomes less bold as more of its flesh is bitten away. The BBC is lucky to get away with just one government clash each year. Often many more. They are all predictable and all solvable. Just.

The 'storm over' usually comes from news and current affairs – just news post John Birt's era. It is the Achilles heel for every DG. Some like George Entwistle and Greg Dyke get crucified on that cross. One stray story about 'Yesterday's men' or '45-minute warnings in Iraq' and political damnation falls on them. Some like the Bashir/Diana affair are self-inflicted. BBC attempts at cover-up almost always fail. Look at poor Tony Hall, now unemployable in a public role. Of the seventeen DGs to date the quality is variable. From the great like Carleton Greene and Mark Thompson to the transitory like Dyke and Entwistle to the simply awful such as Ian Trethowan and Hall. The jury is out on Davie, the first non-journalist to be DG but the early portents are good. Firm and fair.

Current affairs is the cutting edge of the output by its very nature. The outpost of Lime Grove – to which John Birt took a physical ball and chain – the source of many of the rows. Jeremy Paxman once said the motto of the old pre-Birt Lime Grove was: 'How can we piss off the government this week.' Birt may have tamed that spirit of rebellion but he did not dowse it for good. The occasional *Panorama* still can cause quite a stir.

The 'storms' are not always in news either. The conspiracy of silence over the paedophile activities of Jimmy Savile and Stuart Hall – who had a room with no view for young girls in Manchester Broadcasting House – shows the power of on-air talent to simply do the unspeakable and get away with it. Hendy is good on talent power from the early days of steam radio to today's on-air monsters.

At the end of the day, though, the BBC is at heart about making great programmes. Plenty of them across all genres. The archives are testament to that. Great programmes are made by great, creative producers given space to roam their imaginations by managers protecting their freedoms. Birt never understood that. His command and control was much firmer than Reith's.

The BBC survived both. Birt's positive legacy though is much greater. He 'found' digital on the US West Coast and found it early. Thanks to him BBC Online is now world leading as is the clunky but pioneering BBC iPlayer. Throughout its history, as Hendy shows again and again, the BBC has been a broadcasting amoeba moving effortlessly into new unexplored areas. Domestic radio, then the Empire/World Service; television reluctantly at first until the ITV rocket, then entertainment galore; digital online and more recently podcasting. This conquering of new empires annoys the hell out of commercial competitors who are too slow/lazy/mean (you decide) to find new platforms. Their audiences are more sophisticated and do. The left-behinds whinge and try to kill the BBC baby. A classic example: the development of ultra-local digital by the BBC ten plus years ago. Newspapers strangled it at birth. Field clear, they still found their audiences no longer wanted to read and pay for 'ink thrown at dead trees' even online. The local newspaper graveyard in the UK is full to overflowing.

What of the future after the next Charter in 2027. Many in the Tory Party want to kick the licence fee not just into the long grass but out of the park. This household poll tax will need much creative thinking if it and the BBC are to survive in an age of deep pocketed streaming services like Netflix and Amazon Plus. The former has 17 million subscribers in the UK alone. That figure may have peaked.

I have a modest proposal: pin the basic licence fee at a firm and affordable figure. Say £100 per year. For that the audiences get a slimmed-down output on all platforms. Some services like the World Service go to new funding sources. Some simply cut. The licence payers will get first view on all television and radio programmes. Any second views and access to additional sport, drama, entertainment will have to come via conditional access to the BBC iPlayer through small incremental subscription packages. Access to the vast and rich BBC archives too. The boxed sets to end all boxed sets. This hybrid of the public service licence fee and private extra subscription may just save the BBC.

Hendy is a vital tool in any fight for the corporation to survive beyond 100. He is easily the best and most readable BBC historian to date. Buy the book. Force it on your students. It will lift your PSB spirits.

John Mair is a former BBC current affairs producer. Six of his forty six edited book collections to date have been about the corporation. The latest, *The BBC at 100: Will it survive?*, was published by Bite-Sized Books in 2021

REVIEWS

Through her eyes: Australia's women correspondents from Hiroshima to Ukraine
Melissa Roberts and Trevor Watson (eds)
Hardie Grant Books, Richmond, Victoria, 2022
pp 304
ISBN: 9781743798898 (pb)

A confession: I am an academic and a journalist, but the name at the top of an article means little to me – whether my own, or anyone else's. It never has. I am always far more interested in elegantly rendered content. Whether it's written by a man or a woman is irrelevant. This gender disregard may seem counterintuitive. But being a woman does not change the craft of journalism. I know it changes almost everything else, but to survive as a woman in many (if not most) industries needs a sense of bloody-mindedness about our right to be there, and a weary robustness born of battle.

In their preface, the co-editors of *Through her eyes*, Melissa Roberts and Trevor Watson touch on the sexism experienced by all female journalists. Like me, they think and write: 'The gender of a correspondent shouldn't matter.' They qualify: 'But the reality is that until very recently, gender determined all in journalism, particularly opportunity.' This is also true.

Several of the correspondents in this book hurdled gendered obstructions to their career and set out alone to foreign lands, funding themselves by freelancing. So, in many ways, reading *Through her eyes* is humbling. Not because it collects the stories of 29 Australian female foreign correspondents who fought hard for their place, but because it collects the stories of foreign correspondents.

Most of these stories are deeply reflective. These chapters are the ones that resonate most – and will, I hope, make readers truly think. They reflect not on being an Australian woman in the field, but on the job and the skills of journalism. On speaking truth to power through written words.

Emma Alberici's chapter 'What's news?' is the one that really stands out. It's not so much a running mission of gathering news in war-torn, dangerous and corrupt countries, but more an essay on the state of play of news-gathering culture. Alberici writes with a simmering, recognisable fury. She begins with the fiasco that was the Tampa incident in August 2001 – 'one of the most shameful periods in our political history' – and the subsequent spiking of the scoop she and Terry Ross gathered for Channel 9's *A current affair* on Nauru, where Australia dumped 434 traumatised people, most of them Afghan refugees. *A current affair* replaced the shattering and shameful story of Australian government callousness Alberici and Ross had filed with an interview with an inventor who claimed to have created a cure for sweating. After 30 hours of getting to Nauru and manically interviewing, writing, filming and filing there, Alberici tells Ross that back in Sydney, their work has been shelved. Ross vomits at the news.

She writes of 'serendipity' launching her from the commercial Channel 9 to the ABC later that year. Seven years later, she became the ABC's European correspondent. And then there are several eviscerating pages on the Murdoch press, particularly in the United Kingdom, circling the phone hacking scandal and subsequent Leveson Inquiry. It is a verifiable and considered unpacking.

She writes a tad despondently about the Fourth Estate and public interest notions of journalism, and scathingly about how 'media houses continue to undermine the trust bestowed on them'. But she ends hopefully, invoking multi-platform news outlets, writing that 'younger audiences and readers are voting with their feet, taking advertisers and philanthropic money with them'. This chapter is a personal perspective from inside an industry still desperately reshaping and reforming itself. It's cogently argued, with a succinct rhythm.

We all know women are written out of much historical narrative – they have been for centuries. The book redresses this, retrofitting stories of past female foreign correspondents between those of contemporary journalists. These historical chapters – on Lorraine Stumm, Diane Willman, Kate Webb and Margaret Jones – are compiled by editors Watson and Roberts. They are shorter by comparison and told in the third person, so give the text a slight imbalance. But they aptly place these women in the vanguard of Australian foreign correspondent work, alongside their contemporary counterparts.

The arc of this text performs an important function, honouring this work between the covers of a book, patching up and correcting the historical imprint of Australian foreign correspondents. The editors write:

> Women correspondents are the equal of their male counterparts. They are among the bravest and most insightful journalists we have at a time when the hot zone is more dangerous than it has ever been.

They argue that the type of journalism historically covered by female journalists, what they call the 'soft' stories, are now the 'big' stories. This leap, infused with the argument that women report with more empathy than men, is polemical. By making it, the editors inadvertently differentiate between the product that male and female journalists produce. This is less than helpful in chasing equality for women – but I understand it, in this context, as counterbalance.

Each of the 29 stories in *Through her eyes* has the impact of a blockbuster film. There is some powerful writing. Every chapter is an eye-opening glimpse into a world gone crazy – continuously, for the past 80 years. This is my biggest take-away: the ubiquitous corruption, greed, inequality and hatred we perpetrate on each other. The granular lens through which most of these chapters are written is scintillatingly thought-provoking: the current Ukrainian plight; the fall of the Soviet Union; the highly surveilled China; coming face to face with the Taliban; being in Pakistan when a US elite squad executed Osama bin Laden. Beirut, Syria, Gaza, India, Central Africa, the Pacific and more. The stories are as riveting as they are horrifying.

When practitioners lean into their craft and write personally about what they see and feel, it invokes Dan Wakefield's 1966 foundational text *Between the lines: A reporter's personal journey through public events*. Clearly a thinker before his time, Wakefield was one of the first to discuss the story behind the story – the story between the lines on the public record.

This is what *Through her eyes* gives us: the rest of the story, imbued with each writer's personal experience and perspective, separate and additional to what was published or broadcast. It's the journalist's experience of gathering the story: what else she saw and felt.

All the book's chapters are strong and authoritative: Barbara Miller on the Russian invasion of Ukraine; Cate Cadell on technological surveillance in China; Anna Coren in Kabul; Kirsty Needham's expulsion from Beijing; Tracey Holmes in China and the Middle East; Ruth Pollard in Syria; Gwen Robinson in Manila; Sue Williams in Caledonia. It is a stellar cast of gifted reporters: some dodging bullets, some dodging predatory men (including, for Janine Perrett, former prime minister Malcolm Fraser), some getting deported, some running towards the World Trade Center on 9/11 when everyone else was running away. Yes, they are as brave, courageous and insightful as their male counterparts – but that is not surprising to any thinking woman. And it should not surprise any thinking man.

Women historically – and still – are blocked, excluded and obstructed in their careers, personal lives and education (more in some parts of the world than others). Just because they are women. *Through her eyes* offers a significant rebalancing act, for what was once deemed a male province. But what is my real dream? To wrap my hands around a text written by Australian foreign correspondents of diverse identities and genders, within the pages of one book. A balanced, thoughtful and considered compilation of a cross-section of excellent Australian reporting from afar, continuing to speak truth to power through writing.

Dr Sue Joseph,
Senior Research Fellow,
University of South Australia

- First published in The Conversation: https://theconversation.com/bravery-insight-and-simmering-fury-australian-female-correspondents-on-speaking-truth-to-power-189962

REVIEWS

Plagued: Australia's two years of hell – the inside story

Simon Benson and Geoff Chambers

Pantera Press, Neutral Bay, New South Wales, 2022 pp 352

ISBN: 9780645476750 (pbK); 9780645476767 (ebk)

The publication of *Plagued* by Simon Benson and Geoff Chambers is destined to become a classic study of the perils for journalists in writing books about current political events. You might have missed it in the tumult swirling around former Prime Minister Scott Morrison's multiplying ministries trick – but *Plagued* is where the public got its first inkling that Morrison had a yen for job-sharing. By 'inkling', I mean the book had part of the story, but not the most important part. That should ring alarm bells: the main benefit of journalists writing books is they have the time and space to dig deeper into current events to reveal what is not known, or is rushed past, in daily media coverage. The book's revelations are not just politically significant but will surely feature in future historians' accounts of the 2019-2022 Coalition government. So what happened?

Plagued is the work of two experienced journalists: Simon Benson, political editor for *The Australian* (and before that for *The Daily Telegraph*) and Geoff Chambers, chief political correspondent for *The Australian* (previously news editor at *The Daily Telegraph*). The newspapers' owner, News Corp Australia, has a large, well-resourced Canberra political bureau and appeared to have a direct line to the former prime minister and his office. News Corp regularly received speeches ahead of other journalists and broke numerous stories. The company's media outlets strongly supported the former Coalition government, to the point of using its journalism to campaign for it – as academics Denis Muller and Rodney Tiffen have written in articles for The Conversation.

The subtitle of *Plagued* is 'Australia's two years of hell – the inside story'. The back-cover blurb trumpets the two journalists' 'exclusive access to the crucial machinations of government at the country's highest levels, not just within the corridors of power but also behind doors normally sealed'. The promise of taking readers into places normally hidden from their view is territory Bob Woodward of *The Washington Post* has been mining since the 1976 publication of his account, co-authored with Carl Bernstein, of the end of the Nixon presidency, *All the President's men: The final days*. Woodward and Bernstein took us into the Lincoln Sitting Room the night before Nixon resigned in 1974, to see Nixon asking his secretary of state, Henry Kissinger, to pray with him. Similarly, Benson and Chambers take us into the Lodge in January 2020 after Morrison, 'badly bruised by the fierce criticism of his family's Hawaiian holiday', has returned to work and is receiving early warnings about covid-19. The authors describe Morrison stepping out of a dinner at the Lodge with his treasurer, Josh Frydenberg, and the Nationals leader, Michael McCormack, to take a phone call from his elder brother. 'Morrison could hear the dread in his brother's voice even before he heard the fateful words, "Dad's gone".'

What we're offered is a seat in the room where great ones make crucial decisions affecting all our lives. It can be thrilling to read. Watch Nixon as he beats the carpet in anguish, contemplating his political mortality. Listen as Frydenberg tells Morrison early in the global pandemic that the budget surplus is toast and the wage subsidy package is going to cost $130 billion. My God, replies the PM.

There are a number of problems here. First, positioning the reader at the scene of important events is alluring, but how do we know the events are being accurately recounted? We don't. We have to trust the authors. One way journalistic authors can gain trust is by telling readers how they know what they know – and sharing their means for weighing sources' conflicting accounts of events. This has become increasingly common in recent years, precisely because of earlier controversies involving Bob Woodward, among others. There was a lot of debate, for example, about whether Nixon did actually thump the carpet.

A recent example of improved practice in book-length journalism is Patrick Radden Keefe's *Empire of pain: The secret history of the Sackler Dynasty (2021)*. It has 62 pages of endnotes and a five-page note on sources, outlining the thousands of pages of court documents, law enforcement files and letters Radden Keefe drew on (and how he obtained them), along with the number of interviews he conducted – 200-plus. Where Radden Keefe attributes thoughts or feelings to people, it is because his interviewees have told him what they thought and felt, or he is relying on a characterisation from someone who knew them.

Patrick Radden Keefe's *Empire of pain* is an example of improved practice in book-length journalism.

Plagued has endnotes, but they are for secondary sources or transcripts of ministers' media conferences. This is fine, but it accounts for only a portion of the book's contents and none of its insider material. For instance, a series of text messages Morrison sent the Victorian Premier, Daniel Andrews – which range from comradely support ('Hang in there Dan') to an exchange about the Commonwealth and state governments coordinating responses to the second wave of the virus in mid-2020. Morrison and Andrews, the authors report, enjoyed good relations in private, even if they sometimes clashed in public. After Andrews sharply criticised aged-care facilities and health minister Greg Hunt publicly rebuked him, Morrison sent the premier a text saying: 'Am standing up shortly, I assure you my tone will be very supportive … There is nothing to be gained by personalising the challenges we face,' to which Andrews replied: 'Agreed.'

I say 'report'; because the book says nothing about who was interviewed or when. Occasionally the phrase 'Morrison later recalled' is deployed, but that's primarily when he is quoted commenting on past events. It is the only (oblique) sign that he has been interviewed for the book. Very few others – not Andrews, nor federal ministers – are quoted from interviews with the authors, as far as can be seen. Benson and Chambers have not only failed to give readers any idea of the sources of their exclusive material, but aggravate matters by rendering numerous passages in the omniscient authorial voice – as quoted above, when Morrison learnt of his father's death. The omniscient authorial voice is a longstanding device in novels where the author is literally the creator of their fictional universe, but journalists by definition are not omniscient. They deal with verifying the truth of events that are contested or confected or hidden.

Again, it is a common criticism of Woodward's work. The trend in recent works of long-form journalism is to avoid an omniscient authorial voice and practise some humility, drawing attention to the limits of what can be known – and to the writer's own position and predisposition towards the subject. Margaret Simons has been doing this for years, first in her 1999 book *Fit to print*, when she shone a light on the workings of the Canberra press gallery. More recently, when Katharine Murphy, political editor of Guardian Australia, wrote about the global pandemic for a *Quarterly Essay* (published in late 2020), she foregrounded how she was not part of the 'Yes mate' club of male broadcast interviewers chosen by Morrison to reach his preferred public – and neither was her publication, Guardian Australia.

With humility and transparency not in the offing, what becomes clear by the end of *Plagued* is that it recounts the past three years primarily from the perspective of Scott Morrison. The reader is given his version of every event; it is the authors' preferred version. Morrison, according to *Plagued*, works harder than anyone, is across his brief better than anyone, cares more about the Australian people, knows better than anyone what is needed, sees geopolitical trends more clearly. He wants to rise above daily politics and yearns to bring people together – a quality he admired in former Australian prime ministers Bob Hawke and Joe Lyons.

Problems that arise are always the fault of others, from the 'sclerotic', 'folder-bearing bureaucrats' who fail to brief him quickly enough about the crisis in aged-care homes, to overly cautious officials on the Australian Technical Advisory Group on Immunisation, and everyone in between. The result of the 2022 federal election comes as something of a jolt to this relentlessly Morrison-marinated narrative. The change of government is dispensed with in four short paragraphs on the book's final page. A brief explanation is proffered a few pages earlier:

Politically, the prime minister had fallen victim to the longevity of the plague, the elevation of hostile Labor premiers to a national platform, the inevitable mistakes that would be made the longer it persisted, and an impatient and cranky public.

Morrison's own reflection is: 'The only thing I can observe is that our critics are seeking absolute perfection and anything less than that is a failure, and that means the whole world failed.'

If that straw-man-seeking language sounds familiar, it is. Morrison sounded a similar note in his hour-long media conference on 17 August, when he said as prime minister he was 'responsible pretty much for every single thing that was going on, every drop of rain, every strain of the virus'.

It was at that media conference, too, that Morrison pitchforked his obedient chroniclers into the briar patch. He revealed he had given Benson and Chambers 'contemporaneous interviews' where he told them he had been sworn in as health minister alongside Greg Hunt in March 2020. As they report, Morrison and Hunt agreed that checks and balances were needed on the powers of section 475 of the Biosecurity Act. Passed in 2015 under the previous Coalition government, it gave a health minister sweeping powers that overrode other laws and were not disallowable by parliament. Morrison then hatched a radical and until now secret plan with then attorney-general, Christian Porter's approval. He would swear himself in as health minister alongside Hunt who 'not only accepted the measure but welcomed it'. In the next paragraph, they quietly report Morrison also swore himself in as finance minister alongside Matthias Cormann, but don't say whether Cormann knew.

Excerpts of *Plagued*, including reference to Morrison's hidden new powers, were published in The *Weekend Australian* on 13 August. But nobody seemed to notice until nearly 48 hours later, according to a chronology pieced together by Amanda Meade, media writer for Guardian Australia. Then, thanks to reporting by Samantha Maiden of News.com.au and Andrew Clennell of Sky News, it was revealed there was a third portfolio Morrison had acquired – Resources – and that Cormann had not been let in on the secret.

On Monday 15 August, the current Labor Prime Minister, Anthony Albanese, expressed his alarm at news of the secret plan and vowed to seek advice about its legality, and its implications for the Westminster system of government. The issue ran all week, prompting calls for Morrison to resign from parliament and launching a thousand comic memes, which Morrison himself wanted everyone to know via Facebook that he too found amusing.

On Sunday 21 August, Maiden clarified on ABC TV's *Insiders* that it was Cormann who rang Morrison demanding an explanation, rather than Morrison calling his former longtime finance minister to apologise. Something else was becoming clear: Morrison had done a reverse Janet Malcolm, first seducing, then betraying his two journalistic courtiers. He had seduced them with the prospect, unique as far as we know, of exclusive access to him 'in the middle of the tempest', as Morrison put it at his media conference. He gave them the most defensible end of the story – assuming power for health alongside Hunt at the beginning of the pandemic – and another morsel – assuming power for finance.

But no more. Now, Benson and Chambers have no one but themselves to blame for failing to ask more questions. They called it 'a secret plan' and secrets are to journalism what catnip is to cats.

Then Morrison betrayed them by revealing 58 minutes into the media conference that he had told them about the shared ministerial arrangement at the time. It's not clear whether Morrison told them about all five portfolios, and that he had actually overruled one minister, Keith Pitt – on an issue driven not by the pandemic, but the desire to be re-elected. And the authors are being reticent.

Asked by Kieran Gilbert on Sky News when they became aware, Chambers said: 'Well, we spoke to dozens of people over two years and this was part of the story and, well, the story is out now. So that's my response.' If Chambers were a politician bowling up that answer at a media conference, do you think that would satisfy his questioners? The whole tawdry episode brings to mind a famous essay by Joan Didion, where she argued Bob Woodward wrote books 'in which measurable cerebral activity is virtually absent'. That is, Woodward relentlessly accumulates quotidian details – what people eat, what they wear – but refuses to question the meaning of events or discuss the issues he is reporting. She quotes Woodward saying, essentially, he writes self-portraits of the people who cooperate with him for his books.

Plagued is replete with quotidian details: the former PM's official car in Sydney was a 'bulletproof white BMW 7 Series'; early in the pandemic he and Daniel Andrews enjoyed a 'glass of whiskey from a bottle of single-malt Tasmanian lark'. Yet it rarely pauses to question Morrison's version of events – and equally rarely seeks to contextualise events, or consider alternative perspective in any but the most cursory way. On the former, *Plagued* does not mention, for instance, that one of the main reasons Morrison was fiercely criticised for his Hawaiian holiday was because he was secretive about it. On the latter, the issue of gender equality, for instance, loomed large in the last term of government; but it occupies just two pages in *Plagued*.

What began as two News Corp Australia journalists' attempt to secure Scott Morrison's reputation as the leader who steered Australia through the global pandemic looks most likely to have tarnished his legacy forever. That's an eye-watering own goal. When Didion's essay about Woodward's work was published in *The New York Review of Books* in 1996, it was headlined 'The deferential spirit'. For its republication five years later in a selection of her essays, she chose another title: 'Political pornography'. Sad to say, it is a title that could refer to *Plagued*.

Matthew Ricketson,
Professor of Communication,
Deakin University

- First published in The Conversation: https://theconversation.com/in-plagued-journalists-have-traded-their-independence-for-access-resulting-in-a-kind-of-political-pornography-189124

The International Journal of Communication Ethics

Subscription information

Each volume contains four issues, published quarterly.

Annual Subscription (including postage)

Personal Subscription	Printed	Online
UK	£50	£25
Europe	£60	£25
RoW	£75	£25

Institutional Subscription		
UK	£175	
Europe	£185	
RoW	£200	

Single Issue - Open Access £300

Enquiries regarding subscriptions and orders should be sent to:

Journals Fulfilment Department
Abramis Academic
ASK House
Northgate Avenue
Bury St Edmunds
Suffolk, IP32 6BB
UK

Tel: +44(0)1284 717884
Email: info@abramis.co.uk

www.ingramcontent.com/pod-product-compliance
Lightning Source LLC
Chambersburg PA
CBHW080847010526
44114CB00017B/2388